TRAVEL MATTERS

The vital issues of travel & tourism

Wesley Nike 2000

Edited by Chas White & Simon Thorp

CAREL PRESS

Contents

(For up-to-date statistics about travel and tourism see Carel Press' annual publication *Fact File*.)

The traveller was active; he went strenuously in search of people, of adventure, of experience. The tourist is passive; he expects interesting things to happen to him. He goes 'sight-seeing'.
Daniel J Boorstin, 1962

No man should travel until he has learned the language of the country he visits. Otherwise he voluntarily makes himself a great baby, – so helpless and so ridiculous.
Ralph Waldo Emerson, 1833

Travel is glamorous only in retrospect.
Paul Theroux

I travel not to go anywhere, but to go. I travel for travel's sake.
Robert Louis Stevenson, 1879

Whatever else we remember of our travels, we remember our departures and arrivals.
Eric Newby

France is a beautiful country with an excellent road system. Unfortunately it is full of French drivers.
John Lichfield, 2000

He who would travel happily must travel lightly.
Antoine de Sainte-Exupéry, 1939

Brochures the whole truth?

You should be able to rely on the descriptions in the brochures – after all, that's how most of us choose our holiday. So why do our inspectors still find them so hit and miss?

There are no building sites, traffic is almost silent, beaches are always nearby, pool areas invariably attractive. When it comes to pictures painted by brochures, the world is a rosy place, just this side of Utopia. But then a brochure is a tour operator's main promotional tool, and tour ops use more tricks than Paul Daniels to entice you: camera angles that would make estate agents blush, and descriptions imaginative enough to make Jeffrey Archer jealous. Always remember that a brochure is there to sell you a holiday, and, as such, is not designed to be impartial.

Of course, brochures also form the basis of a legal contract, and you should be able to rely on the information they contain when you choose your holiday. But can you? Last summer our researchers travelled with piles of tour operators' brochures to an established short-haul destination – northern Crete – and an increasingly popular long-haul one – Varadero in Cuba. We found the biggest problems are not the euphemisms and purple prose, but the omissions and economies with the truth. Have a look at some of the common issues.

The brochure says 'great views of the mountains' our photographer found something different Malia Dedalos Hotel, Crete.

Concealed construction

As our photo shows, building work was a persistent problem. In Varadero, it was on a monumental scale: cranes towering over the beach, hotels the size of football stadiums going up right next door to existing resorts, and lorries rumbling through town. And yet, such noisy, disruptive work hardly rates a mention in the brochures. Similarly, in Crete, we found building sites aplenty, often crammed in cheek by jowl beside hotels full of holidaymakers.

Empty roads

While brochures do usually mention that a hotel is beside a road, the scale of the problem may not be explicitly stated. The main road along the northern coast of Crete is as busy and noisy as a single carriageway can be. The Irene Apartments in Stalis are 'just off the main road' (Sunset Holidays). Too true – because, in fact, sitting by the pool, you are a mere 35 feet from endless streams

of traffic, so you can sunbathe assuming that the clouds of fumes will protect you from the sun's rays. Equally noisy and polluted was the pool area of Hotel Vasso, Hersonissos, separated from the road by only a low wall and a few bushes. Not that you can tell that from the nice glossy photos in the Odyssey, Sunworld, and Priceright brochures, all taken with the road behind the camera. For a more revealing description, look in the *OAG Guide* – most travel agents will have a copy of this more honest compendium – which says that the hotel

---

The 'brochurese' glossary
Here's a crash course in brochure speak.
'Developing' or **'fast-expanding'** – noisy and dusty, with building works everywhere
'Lively' – Irish bars, English pubs, discos, and all-night music
'Ever more popular' – even noisier and more crowded than last year
'Ideally situated' – beach on one side, council tip on the other
'Due for completion' – still being built
'Just off the main road' – traffic within a few feet
'Once a small fishing village' – now a sprawling concrete resort
'Traditional atmosphere' – themed party nights for tourists

is 'good for deaf car spotters who are in no hurry to cross the road'.

Just as infuriating is not knowing whether you have to risk life and limb to reach the

beach. Many hotels in Crete were on the inland side of the main road, necessitating a mad dash across the tarmac to get anywhere, but few brochures made this clear.

The whole truth?

Visit Varadero in Cuba and you'll find a 'stunning beach of soft white sand that stretches for miles and miles' (Panorama). All the brochures – and we – agree that Varadero's beach is sublime. The trouble is, at one end of the peninsula there's a rather large oil field with nodding donkeys, and giant Bunsen-burner-like flames light up the sky. The only brochures to mention this when we visited were Hayes and Jarvis and Sunworld's *Tropical Shores 98*, but even they failed to say how smelly the oil refinery can be. We checked in the latest

---

The Ropy Copey

Every now and then we come across a hotel that's beyond belief: the Horizontes Copey Resort in Varadero is one such place. It is, in fact, two main hotel blocks, but when we inspected we found that one block – the Siboney – was an empty concrete shell with rubble strewn around, exposed wiring, and open drops. None of it had been fenced off, even though it was all just yards from the pool and within easy reach of children's feet. The Atabey section was still in use, but was barely habitable with its peeling paint, crumbling staircases, and rusting fittings – all with a fine view of the noisy neighbouring motorway.

We found plenty of unhappy holidaymakers around the murky pool. All of them had booked through Cosmos. 'The pool was filthy, the filtering system was not operating, the food served was dreadful,' said one.

'Our holiday turned into the biggest and most expensive disappointment we have ever had.' Another likened the hotel to 'a council block beside the M25 – it needs to be knocked down'. The pity is that for the same money, there are plenty of good hotels in Varadero.

Even Cosmos obviously had trouble extolling the Copey's virtues in its *Distant Dreams* brochure.

The introduction could trumpet only the central location and the all-inclusive system – hardly high praise.

Sunworld has selected the Copey for this year, and its 1999 brochure extols the 'comfortable rooms arranged into two buildings and attractive bungalow-design blocks'. Shame half of them were derelict.

More on the mark is the travel agents' *OAG Guide*, which calls the 'crude concrete blocks', 'basic, dingy and dated'.

---

brochures for this summer and found that only Airtours has changed the text to include a mention of these works. Selective descriptions are all too frequent: the hotel may have a divine sea view, but be right next to a diabolical dump. Varadero is a long, thin peninsula with a superb beach on one side, but a motley crop of power stations, industrial plants, oil works, and building sites – and a motorway – on the other.

Fluid Pricing

Now, you might think that the price given in a brochure is the one you'll actually pay. Think again. While we all know about – and welcome – discounts, the ugly flip side of these is unexpected price increases, or fluid pricing. This is where tour operators feel no obligation to regard the brochure price as the maximum you should pay. In our recent members' survey, five per cent of respondents reported that they had paid more than the brochure price.

There is no specific legislation or precedent outlawing fluid pricing – Regulation 5 of the Package Travel Regulations states only that the brochure price must be 'legible, comprehensible, and accurate'. The major tour operators circumvent this by making it clear in the small print that prices can go up or down at any time before you have booked (increases after

booking are covered by the restrictions on surcharging).

While we think that such price increases are not acceptable, their legality is at present a grey area. Trading standards officers are looking at this issue, but need specific complaints before they can take action. Their most likely course forward may be to take up a case where the brochure price is artificially high and never charged because of false discounting. They think this could be judged as a misleading price indication under the Consumer Protection Act (1987).

Over the hills . . .

Hills sometimes seem to get overlooked. The King Minos Palace Hotel in Hersonissos is up a very steep hill, making the 300-yard slog from the beach quite hard work. But for First Choice the beach is 'just 200 metres away' and for Sunworld it's 'just a 10-minute walk'. Portland is spot-on with a 'steep hillside location'. If you have difficulty getting around, ask your travel agent to check a hotel's location.

We found distances less of a problem. Most beaches really were '300m away' as stated, though, according to Thomson, the Minos Palace is over a kilometre nearer to Aghios Nikolaos than it is in real life. But obstacles like busy roads or cliffs are often ignored: the Anatoli Apartments in Hersonissos are '20m to the beach', according to Portland. True – but only if you are willing to leap down a cliff to get there. Walking around the cliff quadruples the distance.

Invisible views

You may have to pack your telescope to stand any chance of seeing the view in the brochure. We found 'stunning views' of waste ground and 'great views' of reinforced concrete, as well as 'tropical gardens' with little vegetation. At the

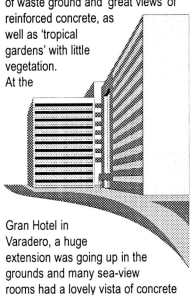

Gran Hotel in Varadero, a huge extension was going up in the grounds and many sea-view rooms had a lovely vista of concrete and scaffolding.

Reading the brochures

Brochures form the basis of your legal contract with the tour operator and must comply with certain laws, such as the Trade Descriptions Act. The 1992 Package Travel Regulations say that 'descriptive matter relating to packages must not be misleading'. Abta supplements these with its code of conduct, which says that 'every brochure ... shall contain clear, legible, comprehensive, and accurate information to enable the client to exercise an informed judgement.'

So you should be able to rely on brochure descriptions: if a hotel is described as quiet, it must be. Likewise, if you don't get the advertised balcony, the operator is in breach of contract.

But we would still advise you to check brochures against independent sources:
● Ask your travel agent to show you the OAG Guide, which has in-depth, honest opinions of resorts and hotels.
● Look at travel guidebooks to the area.
● Read the latest Holiday Which? report on your intended destination.

How to Complain

If your holiday or hotel does not match the brochure description, you may want to claim against your tour operator.
● Be prepared – take a copy of the brochure you booked from with you on holiday so that you can compare facts.
● Complain on the spot to the tour rep. Be polite but firm. Fill out a complaint form and keep a copy.
● Take as many photos and videos as possible for evidence. Videos are particularly good for recording noise.
● Keep a diary of events – and responses from the tour rep. Swap names and addresses with other guests who are unhappy.
● Within 28 days of your return to the UK, write to the tour operator.

For a sample letter see 'How to Complain', Holiday Which? Autumn 1997. Make sure you focus on the areas where the tour operator has breached the contract and show how this affected your enjoyment.
● Be persistent – you may have to take the matter further, ie to court or arbitration through Abta, to get final redress.

FOG WARNING AT SUNSET HOLIDAYS

Sunset Holidays claims to have checked the hotel descriptions in its Summer Sun 1999 brochure against the travel trade's 'truth book' – the independently written OAG Gazetteer. We are left wondering if the tour operator that came bottom of our latest survey read the same edition of the OAG Gazetteer that we did.

Hotel Don Juan, Magalluf, Majorca

Sunset says: 'Palm trees surround the three swimming pools in this pleasant hotel complex'
OAG Gazetteer says: 'a package property way past its sell-by date.'

Samba Aparthotel, Lloret de Mar, Costa Brava

Sunset says: 'bustling, lively aparthotel ... lovely views of mountain backdrops ... a free-form pool is the focal point, set in spacious furnished terraces.'
OAG Gazetteer says: 'huge, tatty and functional concrete property ... contained and a little congested ... wide lawn littered with loungers encloses sizeable Mr-Blobby-shaped pool.'

Sol Ocas/Pelicanos, Benidorm

Sunset says: 'warm, comfortable and friendly ... you'll feel really at home.'
OAG Gazetteer says: 'Busy and noisy ... for those who like mixing with lots of others.'

We recommend that you always ask your travel agent to show you the OAG Gazetteer before you book.

Holiday Which? Spring 1999
Which? and Holiday Which? published by Consumers' Association, 2 Marylebone Road, London NW1 4DF, for further information phone 0800 252 100

Travel Matters © Carel Press

Thomson is asking its customers to pay the 'price of a curry' to ensure quality

Price is back in focus for holiday campaigns

by **Jon Rees**
Advertising and Marketing Correspondent

Actor Patrick Robinson, the voice of Thomson's campaign that it is worth spending more for quality.   *Photo: Thomson*

Thomson has ditched its high-profile strategy of telling holidaymakers the unvarnished truth about its resorts in its commercials and has put price back at the centre of its advertising, so putting an end to its brave attempt to break out of the holiday market's price spiral.

The company, Britain's biggest holiday business, spends about £9m a year on advertising and for the past two years has run a series of commercials aimed at showing consumers that Thomson was different. It was not like those holiday firms which stretched the truth, but instead made a virtue of

'telling it like it is'.

The ads compared the traditionally inflated brochure

'The industry is in a position where the consumer judges on price'

---

blurb with holidaymakers' actual experience. So, rather than a deluxe hotel with smiling staff, the

commercials faced up to what some holidaymakers discovered: a shabby, overcrowded, run-down pile with staff from hell.

In its current commercials for the crucial new year period, however, Thomson has called a halt to this approach and has put price back in the driving seat. The ads feature Casualty star Patrick Robinson and comedian and TV host Roland Rivron telling consumers that 'for the price of a curry' they could afford to switch to a Thomson holiday.

The ads eschew all mention of honest dealing in favour of an emphasis on Thomson's commercial might, which is summed up in the punchline: 'Look after number one, let number one look after you'. Thomson, though, says the ads shift the focus from price to quality.

'The industry has got itself in the position where the consumer judges on price. It is clearly crazy when we're talking about the most important two weeks of the year,' says Shaun Powell, Thomson's marketing and commercial director. 'What really matters is quality, and you wouldn't want to risk that for the sake of a few quid. The ads are confronting people and saying 'think again'. It is a high-risk strategy, but if you really believe in better quality and service, you have to believe that you cannot do it cheaper.'

However, the purpose of the 'tell it like it is' campaign was to set Thomson apart from its major rivals, such as First Choice and Airtours, by showing that it alone was prepared to confront an issue that all holiday companies know is dear to the heart of consumers but which all effectively ignore in their marketing (Trade body ABTA reckons that picking the 'right' holiday would dramatically cut the number of complaints about 'bad' holidays.) The premise of the former campaign was that Thomson's reputation would be enhanced and consumers would be prepared to pay accordingly.

This strategy went to the heart of the entire packaged holiday sector which has been driven by price – not brands – virtually throughout its existence. In an oversupplied market, the holiday companies race to publish their brochures first and establish a lead in early bookings, and consumers wait until the last minute to pick up the inevitable bargains.

'We have never been able to get away from the fact that holidays are perishable products, and we

would rather get a pound for the seat than nothing at all,' says Neil Morris, commercial director of tour operator First Choice. 'All the discounting means confusion. Marketing rules, and there is a danger that consumers do not know the real price of anything.'

About 25% of holidays are sold

in the months running up to Christmas, 35% are sold from January to March, and 40% after April, with at least half the latter discounted.

Industry experts say that vertically integrated groups are suspected of pushing holidaymakers into the capable hands of their tour operators via

---

'We have never been able to get away from the fact that holidays are perishable products'

---

their travel agent chains and on to their airlines, though all groups deny that they promote their holidays to the exclusion of rivals. Nevertheless, there has always

been confusion about which brand customers are loyal to: the tour operator, the travel agent or the airline?

Steve Endacott, group managing director of Carlson holiday company, says: 'Because travel agents would not supply the names and addresses of their customers to other elements of the chain if they were not part of the same company, the tour operators had no way of communicating with their holidaymakers throughout the year.

'So developing customer loyalty through direct marketing proved impossible, and though that's changing slowly, tour operators will still give holidaymakers the 'tarmac wave' at the end of their holiday and will then spend a fortune on broadcast advertising trying to find them again next year.'

Thomson, meanwhile, is keen to stress that it has not abandoned the 'tell it like it is' policy altogether, and its brochures will still continue to include information on customers' own assessments of Thomson's hotels and resorts.

The company will also still fly home and refund customers within 24 hours of arrival at their destinations if they are dissatisfied. Thomson says this latest campaign has its roots in the previous one.

Nevertheless, the key thrust of the campaign is that the difference in price between a Thomson holiday and one offered by its rivals is minimal ('the price of a lobster ... a suede bumbag ... a pair of espadrilles' as the next ads in the series will say).

In order for this to remain accurate Thomson must therefore shadow its rivals' prices closely, which is the way to break out of a price spiral.

Sunday Business 10 January 1999

NEW HORIZONS

You should have taken a year out.
David Jackson never came back and now gets paid to travel.

Travel, they say, broadens the mind. Hard as that is to believe when the images that bombard us all summer are those of Essex girls stumbling blinking out of Manumission into a Balearic sunrise while lycra clad Spanish lotharios snap at their Airmax.

Yet the reality of long term travel is, believe me, a mind expanding experience. You get wise to it. I'm currently on a round-the-world odyssey which has taken me from Chester via Hong Kong to Australia and back to my current resting spot in Hanoi, Vietnam.

So has travel changed my perspective on life? Well, I guess after eating snake in Saigon, singing karaoke with Taiwanese Triads in a seedy Shanghai dive and spilling a redneck's beer in a South Australian one-ass town where I was the ass, then yeah, my view of the world has been somewhat altered.

For instance, I now hate backpackers. They spend all day moping around the hostel, moaning about how they've budgeted for $1 a day until Nepal so can't afford to buy toilet paper and, worst of all how getting a job would disturb their aura as they've come away to find themselves, man.

Not me. Fasting at a Buddhist retreat in Chiang Mai is not my idea of a top weekend. And most importantly, I own absolutely nothing in tie-dye.

Arriving in Hong Kong to find the city so prohibitively expensive that it practically repels backpackers at immigration, I needed work. I found a job with a small publishing house and they promised to sponsor my work visa.

All was fine for three months until, snooping around work late one night, I found my unfiled visa forms leaving me liable for huge fines should I be caught without a valid work permit (mental note – never take a job without a contract in a country where work permits are mandatory). Time, it seemed, to move on.

FASTING AT A BUDDHIST RETREAT IN CHIANG MAI IS NOT MY IDEA OF A TOP WEEKEND

Travelling is a lifestyle choice. Choose travel. Choose bouts of isolation. Choose periods of feeling dislocated from everything – and everywhere you've come to know. Choose meeting great people and making new friends one day to find, invariably, that either you or they or both are about to leave the very next day.

Then there's the sex factor. According to travel legend, the first hostel you walk into will be packed with a bevy of Scandinavian au pairs and Chippendale-style muscle men, all of whom have been lying on their bunks in a hormonal maelstrom awaiting your slightly sweaty arrival. Not so. The person who stocks up on condoms at the airport will doubtless find them more useful for carrying water on an Outback Queensland bush survival course.

Harder though is the certainty that one day you will make that return journey. You get back, head buzzing with tales of strange cultures and alien environments, bizarre characters and new-found friends.

Mark Henley/Impact

And your mates? Well, they've spent the last year watching *Hollyoaks*, going to work and losing at quiz night down your local every week. Nothing has changed. Welcome home.

Going travelling takes guts. Setting out to discover the wider world around us requires a huge mental leap, one that recognises the world extends further than your own realm of experience.

Gimme a life on the road every time.

The Big Issue in the North
20 September 1999

"BACKPACKERS DON'T CARE ABOUT LOCAL CULTURE. THEY JUST WANT TO SMOKE DOPE AND HAVE SEX" by Peter Gruner

The image of backpackers as young, carefree and concerned about the environment is wrong, claims a critical report which says they display no interest in local culture and simply want to establish their own ghettos on the beach, smoke dope, and search out sexual partners.

The report comes ahead of the launch of Leonardo DiCaprio's new movie, *The Beach*, a film about backpackers who inhabit a paradise island and help to destroy it.

It has been compiled by lecturer and tourist specialist Dr Heba Aziz, based at London's Roehampton Institute, for the latest issue of the environmental travel magazine, Tourism Concern.

She describes the shock of a recent visit to her homeland in the Sinai with a group from Egypt's ministry of tourism, where the golden sands of her youth had disappeared under an army of backpackers.

What disturbed her, however, was not the huge numbers of mainly young travellers sitting on the beach, eating, drinking and smoking pot. That's a scene to be found anywhere in the world when westerners congregate together.

The shock was the discovery that this international group of visitors had virtually cut themselves off from the local community, even to the extent of establishing their own coffee shops,

inevitably all with identical menus, with pizza, pancakes and milkshakes. Indeed, there was not an Egyptian dish in sight.

The names of the coffee shops lining the beach of the town of Dahab in South Sinai, which cater for almost 50,000 backpackers a year, gave the game away. With titles like *The Laughing Buddha, Fighting Kangaroos, El Dorado, Al Capone* and *The End of the World,* it was clear that the visitors were unwilling to make any concessions to local people.

"The great irony was that when you talked to them they invariably held very strong views about the environment and the need to protect indigenous communities from destruction and exploitation," she said. "And how were they helping this local tourist community? By totally ignoring and isolating themselves from it.

"The truth was that rather than being interested in the history and culture of the place, they could have been anywhere in the world and it wouldn't have mattered. And these are the same young people who turn their noses up at 'uncool' locations like Spain and the package tour."

The proliferation of guidebooks targeting the backpackers like *Lonely Planet, The Rough Guide* and others have actually created another form of institutionalised tourism, she added.

Dr Aziz is not alone in her views. Sejal Mandalia, who writes in the same magazine, described similar experiences in Pushkar, one of the holiest cities in India for Hindus.

"The Indian tourists who visit Pushkar have a holy respect for the place," she said. "But the foreigners just treat the place as a theme park. They drink and smoke in the temples and show no respect.

"These youngsters are unhappy, dirty and wander from place to place with no knowledge about the country they are in, or respect for the local culture."

Tony Wheeler, founder of *Lonely Planet* guide books, started travelling 20 years ago. He said: "Part of the problem now is that there are so many backpackers. But there is a case for this mode of travel. It brings money closer to ground level, unlike mainstream tourism where the money goes back to the sending country".

"Also backpackers will often go to places that don't have the infrastructure that mass tourism needs. There are a lot of young people out there who genuinely care about the country they are visiting and the culture – it's just at the end of the week they prefer a McDonald's to another curry."

Evening Standard 28 June 1999

Tourists just wanna have fun

I CONCUR with Peter Gruner's article ("Backpackers don't care about local culture. They just want to smoke dope and have sex", 28 June). Being a seasoned "backpacker" myself, I have been appalled and disgusted at the arrogance and narrow-mindedness of many fellow travellers.

I believe the Lonely Planet and Rough Guide series have a lot to answer for. Not only do readers blindly follow the contents of the guides (Lonely Planet's Southeast Asia on a Shoestring guidebook is not called "the bible" for nothing), but I have met travellers who will not eat in a restaurant or sleep in a hotel unless it is recommended in the guidebook. This strikes me as sad. The idea of the "independent traveller" has long vanished, what with virtually every foot of the world being listed somewhere in a guidebook. Basically, tourists aren't looking for an alternative way of life (there is no such thing; after all, "utopia" means "no place"), they are looking for a good time, be it in Ibiza, Thailand, Majorca or Morocco, and for them, that's all that matters.

**Barnaby Attwell,
Rockland Road, SW15.**

Evening Standard 30 June 1999

Why backpackers are better than your average tourist

Young travellers have been condemned as sex and drug fiends. It's just not true says SARAH CHAMPION

This time last year, my best friend Denise and I checked into a 10-dollar communist authority hotel in an obscure town in the Mekong delta. A power cut had thrown the entire town into darkness while we waited for our passports to be handed in at the police station. The dour concierge led us irritably up the stone steps to our room, his candle illuminating a rat scuttling into a corner.

We lay on our beds trying to ignore the bites of bed bugs, the vicious mosquitoes and the sewage odour rising from the river below. In the shower, an inch-long cockroach scurried over the tiles and I found my wash bag crawling with red ants. I didn't know whether to laugh or cry. This was the best hotel in town. Well, it was the only hotel in town.

"Why are we here?" I asked. We'd already been through hallucinatory days of food poisoning in Cambodia and scarred ourselves for life in a small motorcycle accident.

It was a rhetorical question. Like most backpackers we were there for adventure, for excitement, for the unknown people and places and times to come. We were there to escape the boredom of British weather and jobs. We were there for the exotic foods and pungent smells (some nicer than others) and the random craziness of it all. We never made any claims that it was a spiritual journey. We were there for fun, but what's wrong with that? Yes, backpackers are not all angels, and I've met some unsavoury types during my travels in India, Cambodia, Vietnam and Thailand (perhaps only natural as the cost of flights drop and global travel becomes available to all). But I've also met some really cool, interesting people – both locals and backpackers – who will be, if not friends, in my memory for life.

> It's totally unfair to make the sweeping generalisation that all backpackers are drink and drug fiends

It's totally unfair to make the sweeping generalisation that all backpackers are drink and drug fiends with no respect for the culture. It's just not true. It's akin to the hysterical notion of the late Eighties that everyone who went to a football match was a hooligan.

True, backpackers too often follow the guidebooks too strictly, taking the same set routes and staying in the same guest houses. I also admit to having had a fair few wild nights out drinking Thai whisky in sweaty beach-side bars. I was on holiday, after all. But, as well as downing fierce local brews in bars, I have also had many experiences that truly would not have been possible on a two-week package deal. I've been lost in parts of the Mekong delta where no foreigner has been for years; I've been to watch bizarre Thai country and western bands, taken hair-raising ferry trips in rough seas, discussed the UK Premiership in sign language, seen tobacco growing in the wild, seen the ancient temples of Angkor, had water pistol fights with locals during Cambodian New Year, been invited into a school staff room and eaten raw pig salad and deep-fried locusts. I am not alone. Many other backpackers will have had similar experiences.

Having just returned from three months in Thailand, it makes me angry to hear backpackers condemned. The most disgusting behaviour I saw was not from the under-30s, but from the 40, 50 and 60-something men – doctors, engineers, headmasters – supposedly 'respectable' tourists who have no shame about 'buying' local girls by the day or week, parading them in public and treating them as sex slaves.

Yes, backpacking does bring changes in local culture and massive development, and not all backpackers are respectful to local culture, but the same could be said of any form of tourism. Personally, I believe that backpacking has the least negative impact. Package

→

tourists demand monstrous concrete hotels with swimming pools – backpackers live in straw huts alongside the locals.

And, though backpackers may not have as much money to splash about as the usual tourist, they stay for months rather than the usual ten days and, more importantly, their money goes directly into the local economy rather than to the big international companies which employ locals at low wages. Few package tourists spend much money outside their hotel complexes. Backpackers eat at local food stalls and stay in local homes or small hotels. In Vietnam's Ho Chi Minh City, I stayed in a small room above a family's one-room house. The mother explained that the five dollars a night was being used to send her two youngest boys to school. How many package tourists can claim that their holiday money is helping the local economy so directly?

I am a backpacker because I do not take organised holidays. I travel for months at a time and stay in budget accommodation. None of these are things of which to be ashamed. I am a backpacker because I travel with my possessions in a bag on my back. You should try it some time.

Evening Standard 30 June 1999

Backpacking for real

WHY do backpackers always visit India, Vietnam, Thailand and Cambodia? (Why backpackers are better than your average tourist, 30 June.) As a mountaineer I always thought backpacking meant camping, not staying in local flop houses as Sarah Champion does on her travels.

It seems most modern, money-rich backpackers only think they are off the beaten track if they are in the Far East. Having just walked 60 miles across Scotland from Blair Atholl to Aviemore I can assure Ms Champion that I did not meet any regular tourists or "backpackers" except in the towns. Most of Ms Champion's backpackers would not know where Blair Atholl is on the UK map.

Mark Davey, Granville Road, Westerham, Kent.

Evening Standard 30 June 1999

Partying Poms 'make life hell'

Sydney: Complaints are soaring about British backpackers who have invaded seaside suburbs, renting cheap flats and becoming 'neighbours from hell'.

Worst hit is Coogee where stars such as Greta Scacchi have homes. So many Britons are now visiting Australia that the official hostels are full and the partying 'Poms' are cramming into cheap flats.

Theresa McNulty, 24 from London admitted: 'The noise can get a bit much. One lot of mates had a party recently starting on Thursday that didn't end until Sunday.'

Angry Australians have organised petitions but the local council says legal action is expensive. One said: 'It's going to get worse with more coming for the Olympics next year.'

Daily Mail 13 June 1999

All in a good cause

Sponsored adventure trips to the world's far flung corners are an expanding business. John Warburton-Lee looks at the appeal of these journeys and questions the ethics behind them

It is virtually impossible to open a glossy magazine or Sunday supplement without being assailed by advertisements challenging you to stretch yourself on a trekking expedition, cycling marathon or whitewater rafting jaunt in some exotic corner of the globe on behalf of a British charity. 'Bike ride to Hell and Back – 400 kilometres over the moon-scaped lava fields of Iceland' offered as 'A Suckers for Punishment' event by Macmillan Cancer Relief is a typical example. The rhetoric is up-beat and often off-beat. It is aimed at capturing the attention and market share of people who are not only looking for an adventure holiday, but who are also prepared to dedicate their time and efforts to raising money for a good cause.

Charities are clamouring to stake their pitch in this lucrative area of fund-raising with a seemingly endless stream of people wanting to take part in events as far afield as the Great Wall of China or the Namib Desert. Celebrities are also keen to get in on the act. One recent event saw 140 people, including society It girl, Tamara Beckwith, set off on an Enfield Bullet Motorcycle trek for 1,500 kilometres across southern India to raise money for Global Cancer Concern.

The principle of these enterprises is simple. On signing up, the participant pays a non-refundable deposit – the average is around £150 to £250 – and then undertakes to raise a minimum sum from sponsorship – normally between £1,500 and £2,500 depending on the overall expense of the trip. For their part, the charities take advantage of large numbers of participants, off-season fares and inexpensive destinations to run low cost

Raleigh International

operations and thereby maximise profits. The events are designed to be challenging which makes them worthy endeavours to potential sponsors while allowing a personal sense of achievement for the participants, both through their fund-raising efforts and their actual participation in the event. The beauty of this formula is that it makes adventurous trips to exotic travel locations accessible to people who otherwise would not have felt confident or able enough to attempt them on their own, or more pertinently afford them. At the same time the trips provide an extremely effective fund-raising vehicle for charities.

Most charities, directly or through a public relations company retained to market the event and recruit participants, provide the ideas, the support and encouragement during the lead-up period of fund raising before the trip. Methods of raising sponsorship money vary dramatically from standard begging letters to friends and family, sponsored walks and swims, fancy dress parties and curry nights through to more daring head-shaving exploits and blind-date auctions.

Where there's muck

Individual ideas do get more outlandish. I have heard of a farmer who sub-divided one of his fields into metre plots which he 'sold off' for a pound each before releasing his prize bull into the field. The person who 'owned' the plot where the bull dropped its first cow pat won a prize. Surprisingly, while most people admit to having found the fund-raising difficult, the majority exceed their target. So far it seems a perfect partnership, but a question of ethics has been raised, namely is it right that part of the sponsorship money, raised in the name of a charity, is used to subsidise the participant's holiday? Sarah Kitto of Scope, one of the first charities to enter this field and now a market leader, is very clear on this issue. "Overseas events play a big part in Scope's fund-raising portfolio and they are a very successful fund-raising tool. Any fundraising activity has costs attached to it, whether it be direct mail shots, advertising campaigns, organising people to rattle tins outside supermarkets or supervising sponsored parachute jumps. Some activities have a lower percentage cost but they could never generate as much income for the charity over the year as these events do. Added to that we are building a core of long-term supporters who are loyal to Scope. We now have people signing up for their fourth trip with us."

It is a belief endorsed by Sarah Joseph of Mencap. "We expect to make an average profit of £150,000 per trip. We are running 11 trips this year with bike rides in Egypt, India, China and Australia, and a trek in Ladakh and we expect to expand this programme to 14 trips for the year 2000."

The majority of charities aim to operate overseas events on a percentage profit of 60 to 70 per cent. Some of the more ambitious ventures creep down towards the 50 per cent mark but there is a general feeling that anything below this is unacceptable. Some organisations are now finding that certain participants, concerned about their trip being subsidised, are paying their own costs so that all the money they raise is profit for the charity.

For the specialist companies, such as *Across The Divide* and *Worldwide Journeys*, who make the practical arrangements on behalf of the charities – reconnoitring routes, booking flights and hotels,

Raleigh International

planning logistics and providing guides, catering, equipment and safety back-up – these events are big business. Mark Hannaford, managing director of *Across The Divide*, says, "Our job is to ensure a safe, efficient and enjoyable expedition leaving the charity's staff free to concentrate on putting across their message and helping with fund-raising. This is our core business and we are taking a long-term approach to it by investing heavily in equipment and ensuring that we have appropriate numbers of well trained staff supported by watertight operational and safety procedures."

For many people considering the advertisements for these adventures, the big questions are whether this kind of trip is really for them and do they want to spend their precious holiday time pushing themselves to their limit among a large group of people they have never met before?

I personally have taken part in four events. I hadn't ridden a bicycle since I was a child and I'm not a fan of being closeted in a large group of strangers, so I approached the first of these events – cycling in southwest Iceland for Macmillan Cancer Relief – with scepticism. Arriving at Keflavik airport, my misgivings were further confirmed by a number of professional looking cyclists collecting their top-of-the-range mountain bikes from the carousel. One woman told me her bike was worth £3,500. I reflected ruefully that it was about twice the value of my car. I was reassured slightly by the more ordinary looking mortals, even though they were carrying personal streamlined helmets and other such accoutrements of the serious cyclist.

When we reached the campsite all those who hadn't brought their own bicycles were invited to choose one. I regarded my machine suspiciously before setting out on a discreet trial run where I consistently failed to engage the correct gear and ground to a halt on the slightest incline. By the second day, I realised why everyone else was wearing

For many people, the big questions are whether this kind of trip is really for them and do they want to push themselves to their limit among a group of people they have never met?

those fiendishly tight cycling shorts – they are padded.

Saddle soreness and frustration at my lack of pedal mastery were alleviated by the extraordinarily eclectic group I was part of. Will, 18, was a solicitor's clerk from London, forty-something Maureen was a cattery owner, Phil from Liverpool was unemployed and Lucy, in her twenties was a futures broker with Goldman Sachs. She admitted that she had given her address to the man next to her at dinner and was horrified to discover the following day that she had signed up for an endurance bike ride. Always at the back, but with a spirit that was the inspiration for the group, were Stan, 68 and Jean, 63. Stan had suffered a heart attack in 1980 and a stroke that left him speechless for nine months the following year. Four years ago he had lost his wife. Jean, also widowed, had married Stan to whom she had been a bridesmaid 40 years previously. As we cycled along, battling with lava fields and Icelandic

similar. On reaching the end of the Namib desert trek, the ebullient 18-stone pipe lagger from London, the team clown all week, stood with tears streaming down his face. All around people were hugging each other and crying. Most never imagined they could take part in such an adventure or accomplish something so hard and, ultimately, they had done it for someone else.

All of the charities involved in such expeditions agree that the successful formula starts with an exotic location and a stimulating challenge. The market is now highly competitive and growing. Scope, for example, has already filled two trips to Peru next year without advertising and as more charities enter the field, new ideas are being explored. Scope is thinking of expanding its portfolio to include shorter trips with a hard adventurous edge – mountain biking and ski mountaineering in Europe – for which it can set lower sponsorship targets.

Raleigh International

gales, we exchanged life stories until at the end of the week we were allies in adversity and friends. To my amazement, I found I had really enjoyed myself.

Unique appeal

Each of the trips I have made since – a long weekend of white-water events in the French Alps, again for Macmillan; trekking in the Tien Shan Mountains of Kazakhstan with Leonard Cheshire and a trek across the Namib Desert with Share a Capital Christmas – has been very different and each charity and support company has had its own particular style. For all that, however, the impact on the groups taking part has been

Worldwide Journeys is looking at two week trips for fewer people but with higher fund-raising goals: trekking to Everest basecamp, combining ascents of Mount Kenya and Kilimanjaro, and long rafting expeditions. Meanwhile, *Across The Divide* is concentrating on more unusual locations: trekking in Patagonia, coast-to-coast cycle rides across Costa Rica and mountaineering ascents of Pic Communism in Central Asia.

The choice it seems is limitless and rewards for participants and charities are great. Scope had its first wedding last year of two people who had met on a Nepal trekking trip. How adventurous do you feel?

GEOGRAPHICAL – THE MAGAZINE THAT EXPLORES THE WORLD
June 1999

Charity begins in COSTA RICA

'Hang on! You're having the holiday of a lifetime at my expense...'
John Cunningham on the problem of sponsored trips for good causes

National Deaf Children's Society

New century, new challenge. Trek through the Amazon rainforest, go white-water rafting on the Zambezi – or is horse-riding in Mongolia more your thing? Or perhaps an encounter with the 'real' Cuba the lazy tourists never see – on a bike?

No wonder offbeat 'challenges', arduous and expensive though they are, have claimed the smart holiday slot. They offer a unique feel-good factor: apart from a registration fee of around £200, they're free – if you can persuade friends and colleagues to sign up for a sponsorship package of at least £2,500. Two thirds of this goes to charity; the rest pays for your trip. With your new year resolution to

adopt a less indulgent lifestyle wavering in the face of the January sales, there's never been a cannier moment for charities to pitch their fundraising holidays.

Numbed by winter desolation, thousands of us will be sending off for brochures, offering adventures which cunningly mix altruism with exoticism. Packed with jazzy photos, cool prose and 24-hour enquiry hotlines, these brochures are as seductive as those of the big tour operators – except that the word 'holiday' is taboo.

Though the number of trips is limited, exclusive destinations are added every year: the Inca trail in Peru has to be next summer's plum choice.

Your friends and workmates will be anything but bored with your anecdotes and snaps – and impressed that you've raised at least £1,500 for one of the 40 or so charities that run sponsored events.

Indeed, the brochures are almost too successful: it's the lure of faraway places, the chance of moving through picturesque landscapes, meeting remote tribes and seeing ecological rarities that attracts customers. 'I don't think people who do this sort of thing are driven by a particular cause. The charity is secondary to the challenge,' says John Scourse of Guide Dogs for the Blind.

Even so, in the post-trip euphoria,

only a curmudgeonly colleague would dare to mutter that while you have indeed raised an impressive amount for a good cause, you've managed to get a 10-day freebie out of it – funded by sponsors who might not have been so generous had they realised this was part of the deal.

Challenge holidays were the charity world's big idea of the 90s, and chimed brilliantly with the mood of the decade: don't feel guilty about a form of fundraising that's got a built-in bonus for the participants, who work hard to raise the cash and commit themselves to weeks of fitness training for the journey.

But there are growing concerns that it's not always made clear to backers that only two thirds of the money goes to a good cause. It's even less in some cases: Mencap will get just over half of the proceeds of a cycle ride in Costa Rica this year. Airfares, hotels, food, guides and assistance for the cyclists will absorb an alarming 45% of the money raised. Mencap's Sarah Joseph says it's the first time they've been to Costa Rica, and setting up a new destination is costly. Even so, she agrees they've reached the limit with 45%.

The Institute of Charity Fund Managers is so worried about challenges that it is drafting a code of practice to allay public misgivings about an idea that's brought a cash bonanza to many less well-known causes, and attracted younger volunteers to organisations that depend on declining numbers of mostly ageing helpers.

Ironically, the code will be launched just as some charities are forecasting that the popularity of challenge trips will peak in the next year or two. 'There is a need for a code, so that nobody can be under any illusion about how a trip is financed,' says Janet South, who chairs the working party compiling the guidelines. Though most organisations tell participants to spell out how the scheme works to their sponsors, there is a chance of a donor saying to a participant, 'Hang on. You're having the holiday of a lifetime at my expense.'

The code will also advise charity officials, who insist that they need

groups of 80 or 100 to make a sufficient profit, to consider the damage big numbers could cause in environmentally sensitive areas. It will also suggest that charities should pay for projects to help local people, so they're giving something back to the third world destinations they use.

Many blameless charities already do all of this, but to forestall criticism are keen to explain themselves. After all, they have a lot to lose. Take Sense, the

National Deaf Children's Society

National Deafblind and Rubella Association. The chances are you haven't heard of it, as Stephen Bromberg, head of communications, admits. There are about 23,000 cases of this double disability in the UK. Because this is a relatively low number, says Bromberg, 'We're not a glamorous cause like cancer or homelessness.' Two years ago, Sense decided to join the new wave of fundraising, and started with a trek to Nepal. It was instantly successful. 'So far, we've made close to £1m net profit. That's money we wouldn't normally see.'

No criticisms have been made of

> 'It's not an endurance test, but it's not a holiday either.'

Sense, but Bromberg says they have to be totally upfront about what is involved. He's defensive about the effort involved: participants 'are climbing mountains, trekking over

heavy terrain. It's not an endurance test, but it's not a holiday either.'

Of course, charities face a dilemma here. If the hike, canoe journey or horseback trek was too arduous, there would be few takers. And if they dwelt on the poverty of rural Vietnam or Morocco rather than the friendliness of villagers, those on challenge trips would feel like guilty intruders. But it is all presented in the context of wonderful scenery and exciting adventure.

Cuba, one of the first big successes, illustrates the difficulty of what happens when a once-exotic destination becomes too popular. 'We became famous for our Cycle Cuba programme in 1998,' says Mark Astira of the National Deaf Children's Society. The charity has taken 700 people there, making a significant net profit of £750,000 in an annual income of £3m. However, challenge-takers form a fickle segment of the travel market: they want to be wooed with new alluring places every season. 'It's revolutionised our organisation, but I don't think there's any more growth in it. We're stuck on about 400 people this year.'

The word is the same from Guide Dogs for the Blind, where John Scourse says: 'We're planning for challenge events to peak in 2001. Our gut feeling is that there's got to be a limit to this one.'

The challenge bubble is under pressure from two sides. South agrees that exotic destinations lose their rarity value when too many charities go there. She also says sponsors will become weary. 'Early on, it's a novelty. But when the same person comes back a second time asking you to be a sponsor; or when the fifth person knocks on your door with the same request...'

Astira completes the picture: 'There's nothing like a charity for murdering a good idea,' he says ruefully. It's a motto the multimillion world of fundraising would do well to remember. So thinking caps on, while the rest of us prepare to put our hands into our pockets – yet again.

The Guardian 4 January 2000

The Eye of the Hurricane...

...is just one of the weird places people spend their holidays.

Gone are the days when adventure holidays meant driving into Cornwall without a map. Now as Simon Reeve explains, you can fly a MiG over Moscow, go bounty hunting or swim with the sharks unprotected apart from scuba gear

Sorry, but if you thought a holiday to Peru or Nepal would be the ideal way to escape the bleak boredom of Britain in January, you're just not trying hard enough. Today's travellers are turning away from the 'conventional' adventure holidays to tours that are a little more, well, adventurous. It's not too hard to find them either. There are now specialist travel agencies that will organise your holiday to the North Pole, fix you up to fly at Mach 2 in a MiG-25 over Russian airspace, go swimming with sharks or get you face to face with a nostril-flaring bull in true Ernest Hemingway style. There are even companies taking advance bookings for trips into space, although the chances of a discount on that flight ticket are extremely small indeed.

"Great God, this is an awful place," said Captain Scott of the Antarctic, but in 1997 it was the chosen holiday destination of 15,000 people. That might not give Marbella hoteliers sleepless nights but it still represents a fivefold increase in Antarctic explorers in only six years. "Until recently, Kenya and South Africa were just about the only African countries people visited," says Alison Moore of British adventure travel agents Trailfinders. "But now people are going to places like Namibia, Botswana and Zimbabwe. Our bookings for Zimbabwe in 1998 were 25 percent up on the year before." North Korea (the holiday destination for 50,000 people in 1996), Vietnam and Cambodia are among the other growth markets.

It isn't enough for the new breed of travellers to get off the beaten paths (and risk blowing their legs off on long forgotten landmines). Once deep in the Amazon jungle or the African forests, they have to do something really exciting as well, like driving one of the high-powered specials that compete in the fearsome off-road motor rally in Mexico, the Baja 1000. Or steering a small canoe down a very large waterfall. Or strapping a parachute to their backs and jumping off a cliff. When these holidays talk about being a birdwatcher's paradise, prepare yourself for clinging for dear life to a bit of frayed rope over a 500m chasm while a brightly coloured parrot craps on your head. If you haven't thrown up in the cockpit of a World War II vintage aircraft during a mock dogfight, then you might as well have spent the summer in Blackpool.

Nature in the raw

David Gold, an American scientist, is offering two weeks of 'hurricane-chasing' in the United States for around £1,200. Gold concentrates on the so-called 'Tornado Alley' (which includes Texas,

Travel Matters © Carel Press

Oklahoma, Kansas, eastern Colorado and eastern New Mexico) and says: "The chances are good that you will get intimate with at least some of these species of the atmospheric genus: tornadoes (both large and small), striated barberpole supercell storms, 'ice blender' hail cores, and laminar out-flow stogies." The tour fees will cover all ground transportation and lodging. Gold and his partner claim to have seen more than 100 tornadoes, but nothing can be guaranteed during a chase vacation: you may see a dozen or you may just spend your time staring blankly into a stark, grey sky.

David Gold dag8972@ariel.tamu.edu
Tel 001 409 764 8505

A need for speed

If you can't wait for the launch of commercial space trips, why not try a Mach 2 (1,400mph) flight in a Russian MiG-25? More than 3,500 people have already paid Space Adventures (Wild Wings' American sister firm) roughly £6,900 each for the privilege. Essentially a rocket with wings, the MiG-25 was designed to shoot down US spyplanes. It can burn 12 tonnes of fuel as it shoots up to about 26km, a height from which the curvature of the

Peter Marlow/Magnum Photos

Earth is clearly visible. Flights in an ageing MiG-21 or a Sukhoi Su-27 are also available at the Zhukovsky airbase south of Moscow. The downside is that you may blackout and miss everything. Now that *would* be an annoying waste of money.

Space Adventures, via Wild Wings
0117 984 8040

Swim with sharks

Anyone who's watched *Jaws* or seen a fin slicing through the water towards them may find this Caribbean sport a bit stomach-churning. Rather than stay on a seaworthy boat, hundreds of tourists are diving into the seas around Walker's Cay in the Bahamas to splash about with sharks. Conventional wisdom suggests a nice thick cage would be a good idea, but these holidays spurn such comforts. You dive in unprotected apart from scuba gear, and are free to interact and touch the sharks. The Nassau Scuba Centre will even dress your arms in chainmail and get you to feed and play with them. Okay, these are Caribbean Reef Sharks, not Great Whites, but they're still capable of grabbing a pound of flesh if they take a shine to your legs.

Bahamas Tourist Office 01483 448900

Arresting choice

Do you suffer from latent aggression? Ted Oliver is a Briton working as a US bail bondsman: pay him around £800 and you too could kick down doors on a 'bounty hunter ride-along trip'. Oliver runs the National Fugitive Recovery Bureau in Tacoma,

---

What exactly are the bad things? "Well you can get yourself shot," he says

---

Washington. He guarantees that applicants will be taught how to use stun guns, real guns and pepper sprays. You'll even have your own black uniform and bullet-proof vest. "We'll give people a brochure telling them about the good things and the bad things that can happen," said Oliver when he launched the holidays. And what exactly are the bad things? "Well, you can get yourself shot," he admits.

Ted Oliver National Fugitive Recovery Bureau,
Tacoma, Washington

Poseidon adventure

Some of the most unusual (and expensive) holidays can now be found underwater. Last October, Anne White, a retired teacher from Somerset, paid £20,000 to see the wreck of the Titanic, spending 14 hours in a tiny submarine. Legal arguments are delaying other such trips, but there are alternatives. Zegrahm Deepsea Voyages is offering an eight-day £7,000 trip to the Canadian Arctic, in which tourists will descend in submersibles from a dome built on the solid ice to see HMS Breadalbane, which sank in 1853. Brodie-Good of Wild Wings is also trying to obtain permission from the Irish government for tourists to view the Lusitania, the 46,326-tonne luxury liner sunk in 1915 by a German U-boat, 11 miles off the Old Head of Kinsale, Co Cork.

Zegrahm 001 206 285 3743
Focus January 1999

Over the holiday hill?

Michael Kerr says age limits have no place on adventure trips

When I read this week that the tour operator *Exodus* was banning people over 40 from its African overland 'adventures', I thought of Doug. We met last year on a bus in Guatemala. I was spending only 10 days in the country. Doug was halfway through a seven-week trip around Central America. And this at 69, an age when, I thought, men from the Sussex town of Midhurst confined their wanderings to the herbaceous borders.

I giggled at his frumpy T-shirts and shorts, his oh-so-sensible shoes. But Doug was more diverting company than most of the gap-year students I met. For many of them, Honduras, Belize and Mexico had passed in a blur of beaches and bars. Doug had fulsome notes on sights and happenings, better intelligence than the Foreign Office.

But I assume (maybe wrongly again) that he could not have told Posh Spice from Scary, or rap from techno. For those failings, as much as for his age, he would have been disqualified from seven of *Exodus's* overland treks in Africa. The average age of travellers on these trips is 28; the company has decided that, for reasons of 'group dynamics', anyone over 40 is over the hill. He or she would simply not be up to the campfire conversation.

I suppose that goes for me, too. But at 41, I am – the odd encounter with a Doug aside – content with my own company while travelling. I've been abroad often in groups, however, and I know well the benefits of sharing seats and rooms with greybeards.

I think of a wildlife photographer in the Falklands, whose heart needed

steadying with a lunchtime cocktail of drugs. By watching him I learned to take pictures that framed a bird rather than a blur. I think, too, of the 54-year-

old runner in steamy Mombasa, who drew alongside me in our six-mile road race and urged me to slow down. I didn't, and ended up in an ambulance.

Now and again I've been billeted with an old bore, more often with a

---

Ten bonuses of travelling at 40

- You're not tempted to waste money on tie-dye trousers, hair beads and ethnic hats.
- You can collapse into bed instead of on the dance floor.
- If a barman asks you for ID, you take it as a compliment.
- It doesn't matter what colour your rucksack is.
- Hotel receptionists no longer mistake you for the bike courier.
- You don't have to say "Lonely Planet" in a tone of hushed awe.
- You don't need to hang around bars with people who tell you "India is really cosmic, man".
- You can take a fast car instead of waiting for a slow bus.
- You don't get phone calls every 24 hours from your mother.
- You can skip the history sections in the guidebooks – you were there.

---

young one. The former will give you a despatch on every war his trusty manual camera has been through, but he will also let you borrow it when your own is on the blink. The latter will give you a similarly lengthy rundown on the capabilities of his all-singing, all-dancing automatic, but will share nothing but communicable diseases.

Exodus runs more than 250 trips throughout the world, most without any age limit, and says that its policy in Africa is designed to provide 'the best possible holiday for all clients'. But will it? Age limits, surely, are for the sun-sea-and-sex operators and for *Saga*, not for a company catering for 'active, flexible-minded people'. The flexible-minded will need no telling when they're past it; they'll acknowledge it.

Explore Worldwide, selling to a similar market, has no intention of following *Exodus's* example. Its operations director, Derek Moore, is convinced of the benefits of throwing together the young and the young-at-heart, bankers and bikers, Essex girls and Derbyshire grannies. He finds it's not always the wrinklies who wilt: "We get 22-year-olds who expect everything to be the way it is at home and who shouldn't be with us, and 60-year-olds who have fun and verve and spark that would make you and I blink."

Exodus, perhaps, needs reminding of the words of that intrepid traveller Mark Twain: "When I was a boy of 14 my father was so ignorant I could hardly stand to have the old man around. But when I got to be 21, I was astonished at how much he had learned in seven years."

Daily Telegraph 7 August 1999
© Telegraph Group 2000

Travel Matters © Carel Press

18 TOURISTS SWEPT TO DEATH IN RIVER

Desperate search...rescuers hunt for survivors in the swollen river after yesterday's tragedy

"Popperfoto"/ Reuters/ Ruben Sprich

Zurich

AUSTRIA

SWITZERLAND

area of detail

Bern

Wilderswil

18 are killed in a canyoning accident in the Saxet ravine near the Swiss town of Wilderswil

Geneva

FRANCE

40miles

Trip to tragedy ... where the holidaymakers met their fate

Canyon trip disaster

EIGHTEEN tourists were killed yesterday when they were swept away down a river gorge in a flash flood in Switzerland.

The holidaymakers died as torrential storms lashed the area. Six others were injured and three were still missing last night, feared dead.

It is not known whether any of the dead or missing was British. The group were "canyoning", or swimming and climbing down the ravine, when tragedy struck. The dangerous sport — which is banned in many countries — involves "rafting" down rapids in inflatable vests.

It was reported that up to 40 people and eight instructors may have been on the river that flows down the Saxet ravine and the nearby Luetschine river that join at Wilderswil.

Police said the dead and injured were young but would give no further details.

A witness told last night how he watched in horror as the victims were swept to their deaths.

Ripped

He said: "There was a huge wave of water which swept down the narrow ravine.

"Those who tried to hold on to the wall or cling to rocks were ripped free, and then hit by the boulders and debris carried along in the swell."

Jogger Andreas Haesler said he saw seven or eight bodies in the water downstream from where the accident happened.

He said: "When I saw the first body I immediately knew they must be dead. I saw seven or eight bodies. It was impossible to help anyone."

Locals say the river is

By ADAM LEE-POTTER

known to be treacherous at the spot where the tragedy happened — just 12 years ago the town was hit by a flash flood. Last night helicopters were being used to search the Luetschine river.

A spokeswoman for Adventure World — the Swiss holiday firm which organised the river trips — said: "It is a terrible tragedy."

A Swiss police spokesman added: "Eighteen people are dead and six injured. We are still searching for survivors. The bodies have yet to be identified. The survivors are English-speaking but I cannot confirm that they are British."

A Foreign Office spokesman said the survivors were not British, but added: "We do not know at this time the nationality of the dead."

A spokesman for Swiss helicopter rescue service Rega said the death toll could be as high as 20.

Wilderswil mayor Heinz Amacher added: "The river rose in seconds and it was impossible for them to hold on. The town is completely shell-shocked."

The Sun 28 July 1999

"The confused tourist is the softest target for villains across the world" says Simon Calder

WITH HINDSIGHT, the scam is screamingly obvious. You are waiting at a foreign bus station. The vehicle pulls in and the queue moves forward. Your turn to board comes, and a couple of young men push past you and get on. They stand next to the driver, having an altercation and blocking further progress.

A third man, who is in the queue behind you and whom you assume to be just another passenger, impatiently urges you to board. Initially you decline because of the obstruction. But he gets agitated, so you get on and try to make your way through the scrum.

Immediately, he climbs on behind you and squeezes you against the other pair. Then all three set to work, giving your person and pockets a comprehensive going over. Only now do you realise what is happening, and feel trapped and scared. You try to brush them away, but you have only a pair of hands while they have a total of six.

After no more than a couple of seconds, they scramble off the bus and melt away, leaving you to check your possessions and to ask the driver (in a language he doesn't understand) what on earth that was all about. Neither he, nor the passengers, shows any reaction – presumably because the incident appeared merely strange, not suspicious.

Well that's how the week started for me, at Krakow bus station on Monday morning. The gang must have clocked me as I bought my ticket from the former Polish capital to the Czech border. When paying for it, I had handily revealed to them where my cash was stashed. As luck would have it, the money was in a buttoned-up back pocket, which they failed to open. Evidently they also decided that my watch wasn't worth nicking; thank goodness for Timex.

Then I realised that the bag containing my passport, camera, lap-top computer and other traveller's trifles was in the luggage compartment in the lower part of the bus, which was unlocked. Oops.

For some reason the villains had not bothered to grab it – either because they felt that to do so would be to draw attention to themselves, or because they could not believe that anyone could be so naive and trusting as to consign all their valuables to somewhere so accessible to the big bad world. I carried the bag on to the bus, and for the three-hour ride to the Czech border I sat clutching it, feeling insecure and a very long way from home.

The tourist – especially a confused-looking British one – is the softest of targets for villains across the world, particularly at transport terminals. They prey upon the fact that you are tired, uncertain about where to wait for your bus or train, and wondering whether you remembered your toothbrush when you packed that morning. I fear the three men will have targeted the next muddled foreigner who strayed into Krakow bus station that day, and that their mode of operation is repeated across the world.

I was very lucky; no violence was used, and the gang earned nothing for their trouble. It is miserable to lose possessions, whether they are of practical or personal importance. I temporarily lost something, though: trust in the people with whom I was travelling.

Was an accomplice still on the bus, I worried; was the bus driver in on the scam? The joy of travelling evaporated, creating a mist of paranoia that stayed with me across the frontier.

That my mood was not altogether normal became apparent at the railway station, when I heard myself asking for a first-class ticket. The people you meet in second class are much more interesting, but for once I did not want to meet them. (And besides, a first-class ticket for the 400 mile length of the Czech Republic costs just £9.)

I shall try to avoid similar traps in future, and I hope that you may be more alert to the dangers. But what other perils await the unwary stranger in a strange land? Reveal a scam and help reduce the risks for fellow travellers.

The Independent 22 May 1999

The worst ways to lose your wad

Up, up and away

On London Underground's trains, platforms and escalators you are especially at risk from pickpockets. But it's easy to stop them. Hold your bag in front of you where you can see it, or make sure that the clasp is facing towards you. Better still, carry your handbag under your coat.

If you witness a crime ring CRIMELINE and help us put a stop to theft on the tube.

CRIME *line*

FREEPHONE
0800 252525

Policing London's Underground.

London Transport Museum

Watch out there's a pickpocket about in every major city, it seems

Tip-offs about how to avoid the rip-offs that thieves and tricksters use on innocent travellers and tourists

by *Simon Calder*

THIS STORY began a month ago, when three men attempted to rob me at Krakow bus station. When I reported my escape in these pages, dozens of readers got in touch with their own scare stories. (K T Mahon of north London ticked me off: 'You must be getting slack. I couldn't believe you would travel without your passport on your person.')

Everyone agrees that the confused tourist is the softest target of the lot. Several readers report variants of the unpleasant trick involving rogues squirting mustard or worse on clothing and 'helping' the victim clean it off.

Steve Sheppardson of Bromley reports an experience in Manhattan: 'We were sitting on a bench at the South Street Seaport and I had a large camera bag slung over my shoulder. When a group of half a dozen teenagers ran past and around us, I held tightly onto the cameras but thought of it as youthful high spirits.

Five minutes later, after we had moved on, somebody pointed to the back of my jacket and held their nose – when I took off the jacket, the back was covered in a wet, sticky, sweet-smelling mess. At this point we got lucky – an assistant from a bookshop we had been in earlier came out, invited us in to clean up and warned us of what had happened: the kids we saw had squirted my back with something like liquid detergent that sticks and makes a mess. In the confusion, many people would put

their bags down to take their jacket off and are then off-guard while something is snatched.'

What must be the gentlest version of this kind of incident happened to Jane Sinson of Leeds in the centre of New Delhi: 'We were standing near an entrance to the Palika bazaar when two young men walked up to us. One drew attention to a very large piece of bird dropping on my sandal and some on my foot. They took me to a very conveniently located shoe cleaner and told me it would be 150 rupees (£3) to clean the shoe and wash my foot.

The young men were unaware that, although white, I speak Hindi as I have Indian relatives by marriage. I let the shoe cleaner do his work with the young men there, and offered him the going rate of 50 rupees. They tried to protest, at which point I spoke to them in Hindi. They realised they had picked the wrong person, but it is clearly a scam they are playing on unwary tourists, possibly picking on females without a male with them.'

In contrast to this relatively innocuous tale, Andrew Telford of Surrey writes: 'The first time I stayed in Kingston, Jamaica, I was told that if I saw a pole with a hook coming in through the patio ventilation grille trying to hook out loot while I was asleep, not to grab it as it would probably have razor blades set into it.'

Most of our readers' rage was contained within Europe – especially Spain. This account from David Shamash of Oxfordshire is typical: 'My wife and I were driving our UK-registered car into Barcelona recently when the car in front stalled at the lights when they went green – the driver got out and in the ensuing confusion (as we found out later) knifed our back tyre. Naturally we pulled over to investigate the puncture and in the few seconds we were out of the car my wife's handbag was lifted. The police told us that it was a common scam.

Incidentally, having found out how much theft ➡

there is in Barcelona, I warned a friend who was there last month. His car survived, but he was accosted and kissed and embraced by two women in the street who succeeded in lifting his spare cash from a buttoned shirt pocket.'

And Ita Kelly of Hampshire reports an incident that appears typical of many readers visiting Madrid:

'We made the mistake of consulting a tourist map just near the entrance to the Plaza Mayor. A few minutes later a young man walked towards us and dropped some coins at my husband's feet. In the ensuing confusion, a pickpocket took all our money which was inside my husband's buttoned-up back pocket. All this happened in the space of seconds and my husband didn't feel a thing. Luckily the credit cards were in my handbag so we didn't suffer too much inconvenience but we were left feeling angry and paranoid for the rest of our stay. We have not been back to Madrid since.'

From a reader in Washington DC, a warning arrives about Amsterdam: 'The train from Schiphol Airport to Amsterdam Central Station is particularly plagued by gangs of thieves who often work in pairs. One thief distracts the victim, often by asking for directions, while an accomplice moves in on the victim's momentarily unguarded handbag, backpack, or briefcase. The thieves time their thefts to coincide with train stops to make a quick exit.

Within Amsterdam, thieves are very active in and around the Central Train Station, the red light district, in restaurants, and on public transportation.'

Railway stations in Italy can be hazardous, too, according to Barry Sheppard of Brighton: 'I was in Florence and preparing to move on to Venice. I had been to the station to check train times and was walking back towards my hotel when two young women, one with a baby in her arms, approached and thrust a newspaper under my eyes. They jabbered away, pointing violently at a photograph in the paper; I had no idea what they were on about and excused myself with the usual nods, smiles and shakings of head and moved on. Seconds later something made me feel for my wallet which, of course, was gone.

Naturally, the women were nowhere to be seen, but a man was hurrying towards me waving my wallet aloft!

My first reaction was that this was somehow all part of the scam. He turned out, however, to be a Florentine who had seen what was happening and had managed to grab the wallet back from the women before they could hand it over to their minder. All it cost me was a Campari and soda.

The Independent 3 July 1999

The Professional Pickpocket

Every day, some 190 tourists surrender their cash to Venice's most successful and profitable trade – picking pockets. Sabo, 54, from Romania, is a professional pickpocket who works the city. On average, he earns between 30 million and 60 million Lire ($16,500-33,000) a month. 'The best victims are Japanese. They carry lots of money and don't scream. It's not uncommon for a Japanese to carry around 15 million Lire ($8,260). Along with Americans and Germans they're the richest and the least alert. We don't rob Italians. They shout and don't keep much in their pockets. We live in at least three-star hotels where we're not likely to be found, and work in teams of four or five. We choose a victim, follow them until they buy something, and see if their wallet's full and where they keep it. When they arrive in a narrow, crowded place, two 'plugs' move in and walk right in front of them. It's their job to slow the victim down, so they pretend to look in a shop window or ask for information. Then the thief can slip a hand into the victim's bag or pocket and find the money while another member of the team covers his move, using a sweater or a map. There's a fifth member who acts as a lookout, and the stolen money is passed to him. The thief gets two-thirds of the takings, the rest is divided in equal shares. But sometimes there's a boss in control, who will buy a thief for 50 million to 100 million Lire ($27,450-54,900) and then build a team around him. The credit cards have to be used within a couple of hours. We have special people doing this. They shop accompanied by a good-looking woman – young and elegantly dressed in designer clothes. We resell the items at half-price and they get 50 per cent. Some shopkeepers have an agreement with us. They make us a fictitious sale for 10 million Lire ($5,488). We pay with the stolen card, and they keep 60 per cent. Who'd turn down a deal like that? I've got everything – a house worth 600 million Lire ($330,000), a car for me and my wife, a decent bank account. Advice to tourists? Stay at home.'

From Colors 33, Venice p38

RIP-OFF ANECDOTES

Craig Mitchell

ONE READER, who requests anonymity, outlines an entire repertoire of rip-offs.

Spanish Steps
Most crime against tourists in Madrid doesn't include violence, but it is so blatant it'll take your breath away. If you see anyone in summer wearing a poncho or carrying a large garment over their arm, beware – it's almost sure to hide a hand for slipping into someone else's pocket.

On a bus
Once I was on a crowded bus outside the Prado. Five people were jostling me, and I only realised what was happening when I saw a hand going for my inside jacket pocket. The five were middle-aged and wore suits.

On the Metro
The classic: they nick your bag as the door closes, and jump off.

In a restaurant
Many places have a lot of tables in a fairly small space. Some women put their handbags over the top of the back of their chair. The thief sits down at a table near a hanging bag and goes through it.

Sitting on a bench alone
Two varieties here: you are reading or relaxing. Two women walk up to you: one has a baby. She thrusts the baby into your arms as they go for your bag. The other trick: someone approaches you and starts talking. They get your attention while someone behind you goes for the bag.

Where to avoid
Areas such as the Plaza del Sol, the Plaza Mayor and, of course, the Rastro, the flea market area. One thief who I saw apprehended by a member of the public in Sol and frog-marched to a policeman, was let go when the policeman wasn't interested.

One exception was a thief who must have been new to the city. He stole a bag on Calle Toledo and ran towards the little streets near Plaza Mayor. There are always policemen outside the fire station there, and he ran straight into their arms.

The Independent 3 July 1999

You want to be a woman alone, but are you safe?

Maggie Moss offers some golden rules: remember the three Cs - Compromise, Common Sense and Confidence

Fear of what might happen when travelling alone in a strange land narrows the horizons of many women. They take uncomfortable beds, insanitary loos and plain inconvenience in their stride. But fear of attack, sexual harassment and illness often prevent them from visiting many destinations.

These are compounded by the lurid tales friends invariably recount when a woman declares her plans for a trip to somewhere out of the ordinary. These stories always involve the friend of a friend of a friend.

In reality, travel need be no more dangerous for a woman than for a man. But a woman's experience can be different, sometimes surprisingly so.

Two friends once compared their visits to Istanbul. Both enjoyed the city, fended off carpet vendors at every street corner and were hassled by strangers offering themselves as guides.

He had never noticed that the cafes were virtually male-only; he had never felt conspicuous ordering a meal on his own; and he sought out the night life without a second thought. She found officials helpful and polite (he found them confrontational) and she easily visited Turkish families in their homes, which were usually out of

bounds to unattached men.

Like all women, in my travels I have had moments when I wished I had never left home. On my first trip to Delhi, I stupidly accepted a 'favour' from a young man I had met earlier. He was pleasant enough, so I took up his offer of a lift on the back of his bike. I spent a

'Like all women I have had moments when I wished I had never left home'

sleepless night, unscathed but uncomfortable, the centre of much attention locked inside an all-male hostel miles from the city centre.

Sometimes travellers find themselves in dangerous situations without warning. The answer is to think fast and get out. In Peshawar, northern Pakistan, I heard shouting in the streets and found myself caught in a surging crowd. I saw a line of police unslinging their weapons. I was thumped as I tried to get out but managed to find the shelter of a wall

before the firing started.

Despite the potential pitfalls, women travellers often find themselves on the receiving end of great kindness and hospitality, provided they follow the golden rules for safe and happy travel: compromise, common sense and confidence.

Mark Henley/Impact

Compromise

You must make an effort to respect local expectations about women, especially outside the West.

- Check out what is acceptable clothing in the countries you plan to visit. Shorts, short skirts and microscopic tops are offensive and will invite problems in Muslim countries; they are against the law in Sudan and Iran.
- On the beach wear a modest one-piece and keep a pierced midriff out of sight. Topless bathing can cause offence in Greece, India, Sri Lanka and other popular destinations.
- Don't attempt to visit an all-male bar on your own:

you will attract unwanted attention, even hostility. Better to talk to local women instead, perhaps on the bus or at a market.

- Follow the advice of local women, even if it means that you have to accept that there will be places that remain out of bounds.

Common Sense

Most British women are already experts in the art of safe travel: they avoid dark underpasses and empty railway carriages. When travelling you must anticipate potential problems.

- Never arrive in a new city after dark. Make sure your first night's accommodation is booked ahead.
- Team up with other travellers before going into wilderness areas.
- Take account of the greatest danger you will face anywhere: traffic accidents.

Confidence

Confident travellers give out clear signals that they know what they are doing and where they are going.

- Do your homework. Most of the popular guides have sections for women. Look out for other travellers and take their advice.
- Get a feel for local ways and be quick to adapt.
- Learn to ignore minor hassles (including the odd wolf whistle and comment), challenge unacceptable behaviour and trust your intuition.

The Guardian 24 January 1999

Holiday Trade

Everyone's second reaction to the earthquake in Turkey – after empathising with the victims – is to wonder whether it is safe to go on holiday there. It is an obvious if rather selfish thought, but one being asked increasingly as tragedies strike a growing list of countries on the tourist map – countries whose economies depend in part on the growth of the travel industry.

However while Turkey's ministry of tourism has got the biggest current headache, as it ponders not only the reconstruction of those parts of the tourist infrastructure (mainly in Istanbul) damaged by the quake, but the rebuilding of confidence by foreign tour operators, there has been other bad news demanding attention.

Huge media coverage of the first anniversary of the Omagh bomb can't have done much for tourism in Northern Ireland; and the kidnapping of four European tourists in Iran a few days ago has been a blow, officials concede, to their country's fledgling tourist industry.

Go back a little further to hurricanes in the Caribbean, kidnappings of tourists in the Yemen, earthquakes in Italy and it seems that making the world safe for tourists is a priority for many governments already burdened with other, more pressing problems.

Tourism matters to the economy of virtually every country – even those that seem unlikely destinations will attract the traveller seeking something unique or at least different. It is beginning to matter in Bangladesh, once dismissed as an economic basket case. And, of course, it counts in first as well as third world nations. For Scotland and the Republic of Ireland it is 7% of GDP, for instance; but only 1.9% for Northern Ireland, thanks to the troubles.

But along with the disaster in Turkey – visited by 1m Brits a year – recent days have also brought good news from places where tourism has been devastated. The United States, which pulled out of Vietnam after its

humiliating defeat in 1975, reopened its consulate-general in Ho Chi Minh city – signalling that trade and tourism have the official blessing of Washington.

And two years after westerners were scared away from Egypt following the massacre by Islamic extremists of 58 tourists in Luxor, Thomas Cook Holidays has just announced that its sales this year have returned to 1997 levels. Egypt's tourism receipts hit a record £2.3bn in 1996-7, but dropped to £1.8bn after the killings.

It is impossible to forecast how long the shadow of a natural catastrophe (floods, earthquakes and hurricanes are the most common; they also have the widest effect on infrastructure), accidents (major train or plane crash), wars or acts of terrorism (bombings, kidnappings, shootings), will last.

Firm action against Islamic terrorism seems to have worked in Egypt. "Visitors have been tempted back since security was stepped up in popular tourist spots," says Simon Laxton, general manager of Cook's. "This remains a way of life, but it is in no way intrusive."

However, there is no magic formula for restoring the fortunes of the sector in any country where it

has been shattered. Big discounts by tour operators and the opening up of new attractions are starting to do the trick in Egypt. A timely find of 100 mummies in the Western Desert, many wearing the gold masks of high-ranking Roman Egyptians, has helped as a huge advertisement for Egypt's amazing heritage; so has the development of the country's Red Sea coast as a popular destination.

Such mixed bags of luck, official policy and the swings of the market tend to ensure the eventual return of foreign visitors, however bad the events which drove them away from the sunspots or heritage sites. Even the ravages of a war as terrible as the conflict in South-east Asia start to give way to a legacy in which tourism can be contemplated again – and the enemy welcomed back as camera-toting nostalgia freaks.

But even in Vietnam, tourism is a two-way business. The US expects to issue 150,000 visas a year to allow Vietnamese to visit relatives in America. It has taken almost 30 years since that war for the first guidebooks to Vietnam, Laos and Cambodia to appear in the west – intrepid solo travellers leading where package tours will follow. But the same pattern does not always apply.

The conflict in former Yugoslavia was shorter and more recent – and involved a destination very popular with the British. But the experience of Croatia's tourism industry shows just how difficult it can be to get the numbers of visitors to rise again. In 1990, the last year before independence, about 500,000 UK tourists holidayed there. By 1996, the conflict over, that had dropped to just 31,000.

> **Some countries, popular before wars engulfed them, have tried to make a virtue of their battle scars**

Valiant efforts by the authorities to let visitors know that Dubrovnik has been restored to its beauty and that the coast and islands were safe again, were enjoying modest success: 80,000 Brits were expected this year. But then Kosovo erupted and, though not involved in the conflict, Croatia is again suffering from the drop in tourist numbers: they are staying away in droves.

Some countries, popular with tourists before civil or regional wars engulfed them, have tried to make a virtue of their battle scars. There is nothing like peace, of course; and after the ceasefire in Northern Ireland, there was a huge jump in tourist numbers. This has since levelled out at about 1.5m annually.

Much effort, by way of EC and British government grants, has gone into improving facilities for visitors – from renovating rural cottages for holiday lets to massively increasing the number of hotel rooms in Belfast. Along with this, tourists wanting to get a whiff of the landmarks of the conflict that began in 1968 can, thanks to the enterprise of Ulsterbus, take a trip on what it bills as a 'Living History' tour.

However, there is no demand for the trip beyond the two afternoons a week on which the tour runs. Maybe that proves what several experts in the travel business say about punters' attitudes to places hit by calamities: when it comes to holidays, the public have very short memories. Maybe that is just as well.

The Guardian 19 September 1999

'We have a problem with our port engine...'

Ivor Williams relives his fear of dying when he finds himself in an aircraft emergency after a change of flight

BING! **"Ladies and gentlemen, this is your flight captain speaking. As most of you will have gathered, all is not well with this flight. We have a little orange warning light in the cockpit here flicking on and off, which tells us we have a problem with our port engine"**

A hush descends over the Boeing 757 aircraft, the 15.25 flight BA2641 from Athens. People behind and to the side of me start sobbing, several others make a dash for the lavatory.

My thoughts immediately spring back to an emotional goodbye with Joy, whom I had met on a cruise on the Black Sea from which I am returning.

Joy had left on an earlier flight to Amsterdam, where she lectures. When she turned round for the final wave and smile before heading for the departure lounge, I wondered if I really would see her again, despite the fact that we had made tentative plans to meet in Amsterdam in three weeks.

A lump fills my throat. Now I definitely wouldn't see her again. I wouldn't see anybody again. I was going to disappear in a ball of fire.

"I'm sure it's nothing, really," the captain goes on, **"probably just a loose wire. For safety reasons, it's best in these situations to shut down the engine and return to Athens airport. This aircraft is perfectly capable of running on one engine, so we should have no problems landing. Thank you."**

So just how serious is this? He's got to say that, even if it's far worse than just a loose wire.

I've flown dozens of times and I knew before the announcement that something was up.

We were 30 minutes or so into the flight and we had been circling the Corinth canal for most of that time.

Why me? It wasn't even my flight ... why did I catch this earlier flight, what would I have done with those four hours saved?

A big American to the side of me looked over, pursed his lips and raised his eyebrows slightly. A former military man, he must have been in some tight corners at times, but maybe nothing he couldn't do something about.

I acknowledged him silently and stared out of the window again. That cursed Corinth canal.

A member of the cabin crew came up to me. I was right next to the emergency exit.

"In an emergency situation," she said drily, **"pull the handle down sharply and push the door hard out to the right. You'll be first out."** This did not reassure me much.

BING! **"This is your flight captain speaking. I can assure you that everything is going to plan.**

We've got to burn off a few tons of fuel before we can land again at Athens, which will take an hour or so.

We're going to fly fairly fast. Also, shortly you'll hear some thumping sounds as we lower the undercarriage.

This is to create more drag on the aircraft, which will burn up fuel more quickly.

I promise to keep you updated on developments."

So now we're burning up fuel so that when we try to land and get blown to oblivion, we don't take the whole of Athens airport with us.

Maybe I was getting irrational. Did it matter if I was? Did anything matter? What about that other engine..? It was 101°F in the shade in Athens today – it's got to be overheating by now.

I stared at the emergency exit, a cold sweat creeping over me, then out of the window yet again. I knew every inch of the Corinth canal by now.

The aircraft was still silent, save for the muffled sobbing from various quarters. My mood was swinging wildly from total pessimism to cautious optimism and back again. Is this really it, then?

My mind flashed back quickly. I had escaped possible death several times before.

In 1973, on my way to the Daily Telegraph, where I was working, I walked past a car containing an IRA bomb moments before it went up outside the Old Bailey. I was blown forward but unhurt.

Last year an acute lung infection nearly had me. And several years before that I nearly drowned in a waterlogged wetsuit having lost my surfboard in a rip tide off Newquay.

That same year a gust of wind nearly blew me off a cliff in Dorset.

And my diving buddy brought me up from a depth of 108ft when I ran out of air while scuba diving off Lanzarote. And now this.

My guardian angel's surely done enough already. But, please, one more time?

BING! **"Ladies and gentlemen, this is your captain again."** Was his voice wavering towards the end? **"We should be landing at Athens airport in about 25 minutes. Everything is going according to plan – please be aware of the safety procedures. When we land, we will be followed down the runway by fire tenders and ambulances – this is normal procedure."**

Only 25 minutes until the nightmare would end, one way or another. It would seem like 25 hours.

Pessimism set in again. My diving buddy can have my MGB, he knows that. My house – it's in an even worse mess than usual. Someone will have to sort it all out. And no will, no executor, no nothing. Do I care?

It was dead silent as we approached the runway, not a whisper from anybody – even the sobbing was put on hold. Everything seemed curiously normal.

Lower, lower, then a heavy rumble as the tyres hit the runway. We were down. The fire tenders and ambulances raced after us. We were slowing, slowing.

We had made it.

Huge sighs of relief all round, then the aircraft erupted into a spontaneous burst of thunderous applause and cheering for the captain and crew. Cries of anguish turned to cries of joy. The nightmare ended. I had escaped death again.

The fault put the aircraft out of action until next morning; BA bussed us to the five-star Intercontinental Hotel in Athens for the night, evening meal, drinks and breakfast included. Most of us were indeed ready for a stiff drink.

The following afternoon, after a flawless, one might even say boring, flight home, Joy phoned me to see if I got home quickly and safely. I explained everything. I had been home just 10 minutes – 18 hours late.

The date of that awful experience was Friday August 13.

Financial Times 8 January 2000

26-stone passenger complains over fat surcharge

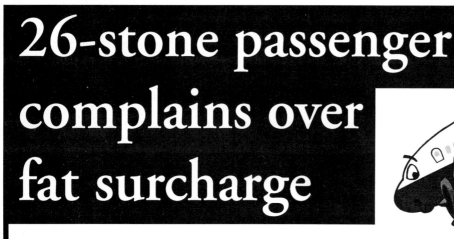

JULIAN NUNDY In Paris

A 26-STONE Frenchman has lodged a legal complaint against Air France because the airline refused to let him board a flight to China unless he bought a second ticket.

Jean-Paul Touzé, 49, a chess federation official headed for Beijing to help judge the Women's Chess Championship in China, said he was told he had to buy a second 7,500 franc (£750) ticket to board a Paris-Beijing flight on Wednesday.

He immediately lodged a complaint with the airport police and the French human rights federation. Promising to take the case to the European Court of Human Rights in Strasbourg as well, he finally left Paris yesterday after buying a second ticket.

The incident followed a refusal by an Air France captain last month to allow a man aged 44 with Down's syndrome to board a domestic flight and join his parents on holiday in Brittany. The captain insisted on a medical certificate stating that the passenger was capable of travelling unaccompanied.

The man who had been taken to the airport by his brother and, according to his family, was used to travelling alone, was allowed to fly on another plane the following day.

Mr. Touzé said he had informed Air France of his corpulence when he made his booking and had been advised to book, and pay for, two seats.

He said he refused because he had never before been obliged to pay double. 'The passenger is paying for a second seat because he is occupying it,' said Michel Folliot, an Air France official. 'It's a security problem and we can't take any risks.'

The Scotsman 14 August 1999

HOTEL BOSS BOOTS OUT DISABLED BILL

BY JAMES EISEN

A HEARTLESS hotel manager asked a disabled holidaymaker to leave because he was 'not the right sort' of guest.

Bill Smith, 56 – who has a mild form of cerebral palsy – was astounded to be told he would be better off in a nearby residential home.

Manager Chris Owen even drove him there. But proud Bill – who has followed the England cricket team round the world – refused.

Instead he asked to be taken to a coach station where he caught a bus home to Buckinghamshire after just one day of his two-week holiday in Torquay, Devon – home to TVs Basil Fawlty.

Bill paid £26 for a single night at the Lindum Hotel. He said: 'I've never been so treated so badly.'

Manager Owen said: 'We were not aware of his condition before he arrived. We don't have the facilities to cope.

'He had told us he needed his food cut up but he hadn't told us he had cerebral palsy. We notice other guests shielding their eyes from people like this.

'They are on holiday and do not expect to be in a disabled environment. He is not the right type of guest for us.'

James Ford, of national cerebral palsy charity Scope, said the Disability Discrimination Act made it unlawful to refuse service to anyone because of their disability.

A Torbay Council spokesman said the claims were being investigated and there would be a statement next week.

News of the World 12 September 1999

Benefits of Benidorm

This Spanish town is much more than a Costa del Cheapo, Derek Workman discovers

In this DisabilityNOW feature we look at European trips and what to check out if you plan to take a carer

Benidorm has become something of a Mecca for those wanting a holiday in the sun who can feel reasonably confident that the pleasures they seek are more or less accessible.

Luigi Bagnoli, mainland holiday services manager for Thomson Holidays in Spain, was surprised by the results of a company survey. It showed that over 8,500 wheelchair users were travelling to Benidorm.

'People who have some kind of disability are booking more and more winter holidays, but it wasn't until we looked at the statistics that we realised just how many came,' he says.

When the UK number one tour operator begins to realise the potential of this market, it isn't long before the local hoteliers become aware of it too.

Why does Benidorm rate so highly as a tourist destination for disabled people?

Apart from the obvious climatic benefits, the answer is simple. Stand at the topmost end of Playa de Lavante and look south to the tip of Ponente Beach. There's five kilometres of flatness, broken only by the hump of the old town and the warren of streets surrounding the Church of St James.

Also, a number of support services have sprung up.

Chrissie Robinson, for example, runs the British Hire Service which specialises in providing wheelchairs and ancillary aids to disabled people. Chrissie says: 'In the beginning, the hoteliers didn't want disabled people in their hotels because they thought the able-bodied visitors wouldn't want to see them. It's completely different now, and people are coming because they know the facilities are here'.

Perhaps this says more about the attitude of your average British tourist. The Spanish people themselves are extremely tolerant and helpful.

This helpfulness came as a bit of a surprise to Norma Crow, who travelled from the north east of England. On the first day of her third visit to Benidorm last year, she tripped over a kerbstone and tore a ligament in her leg. 'I was hobbling on crutches one day, trying to cross a street, when a Spanish man walked into the middle of the road, held his hands up, and stopped all the traffic till I crossed. You wouldn't get that in Tynemouth.'

The visual images of access for disabled people are those provided for wheelchair users: ramps, wide doors, long stretches of flat surface. But perhaps *ONCE*, the powerful organisation which represents the interests of Spanish visually impaired people, may have had an influence too. As Alan Provin, an English visitor who is registered blind, commented: 'If there isn't a voice for people to ask for these things then they'll never be given.'

On his second visit to the town last year, Alan was very pleased with the help and assistance he was given. 'In our hotel there are special tables set aside for disabled people marked with a wheelchair symbol. Sometimes I get a few strange looks because people don't always see my white stick and it can be embarrassing, but overall I like the idea.'

Like many disabled visitors, Alan and his wife Pat have found the town highly accessible and are now considering an extended stay.

Most disabled British holidaymakers travel on package tours and are happy with the support they get from the tour operators. But there will always be people who want the freedom of independent travel. 'That's one of the most important things for both pride and independence,' said Chrissie Robinson. 'I have a client with multiple sclerosis and she wants to go shopping when she wants to go, and she can only do that with the aid of an electric scooter. So I supplied her with one, and I'm going to buy more.'

Perhaps an image which encapsulates the accessibility of Benidorm was the elegantly dressed elderly lady, casually strolling along the promenade at Lavente beach, her chiffon scarf gently blowing in the breeze, supporting herself on a Zimmer frame with wheels. A diamanté studded evening bag was balanced on the crossbar.

It is unlikely that she considered herself disabled, but the features which enhance the pleasures of a wheelchair user also allowed her to take part in the *paseo*, that delightful activity which is so much a part of Spanish life.

Chrissie Robinson, British Hire Service, mobile: (0034) 929 985 801 or 919 413 894
Luigi Bagnoli, regional holiday services manager, Thomson Holidays, tel: (0034) 65 872754 fax: (0034) 65 852189

DisabilityNOW February 1999
Tel: 0207 619 7317 to obtain a free copy of the magazine

Days on a 'beer boat' – a night in the cells

truckers who drive tourists overland and students tell tales to
Amy Shuckburgh

Alice Blacker was a form teacher in Kenya's Rift Valley. Many old pupils still write to her

Alice Blacker *was 19 when she travelled and taught in Kenya with her best friend, Clody Wright.*

Africa is almost completely ignored by other gap-year travellers, so it felt like our own discovery. Going with a friend gave me confidence, but we still couldn't let our guard down at any time.

Clody and I taught with two other girls in Kituro Primary School in Kenya's Rift Valley. I was the form teacher for one of the boys' classes, teaching English to ages between eight and 12 years. Quite a few of them still write to me, which is wicked.

I also taught music to a mixed-age class of up to 100 pupils. We were all given a lot of responsibility and it was fulfilling – although it sounds cheesy – to see children developing and improving their English over our three and a half months.

Clody and I were lucky because we worked in a very poor primary school and the other teachers clearly valued and wanted our help. Other gap-year travellers we met worked in well-off secondary schools where they weren't really needed or wanted.

The school got £80 of the fee we paid to Africa Venture and we helped decide what the money was spent on. The school had very few materials, and textbooks were almost non-existent.

I would absolutely love to do it all again and probably wouldn't change anything about the whole experience.
*Alice and Clody each paid **Africa and Asia Venture** £1,200 each to arrange placements at Kituro Primary School in Kenya. They paid for their flights separately.*

Hannah Shuckburgh, *18, had complete freedom travelling alone on a round-the-world ticket.*

When I arrived in Sydney, Australia, it was a relief after India and Nepal to feel I could let my guard down a bit. This felt much less foreign, with hordes of backpackers everywhere. I had a ticket to do the Oz Experience, a bus which follows a set route around the country.

But I soon began to feel miserable and frustrated at being herded along with others just like me. So, without thinking what I was doing, I got off the bus at a night stop in New South Wales and didn't get back on.

We had stopped at the Dag Sheep Station. I got a job as a 'rouseabout', or dogsbody, shovelling sheep dung and helping out with the shearing. I wasn't paid, but I got a bed and food.

I fell madly in love with the stockman, who re-taught me to ride, and took me to live with him in Nundle, 10 miles from anywhere. It was a mad, romantic existence, looking after his house and horses while he worked as a horse-whisperer. I easily forgot my other, 'real' life.

After six months, however, I had a panic attack. Memories of home that I had been blocking out flooded back. I suddenly remembered what I was supposed to be doing, and practically ran away.

I'm glad I came back, but part of me still longs for that other life. Some people, I hear, never come home.
Hannah's round-the-world ticket cost £1,000 from STA Travel.

Adam Keeling *was 18 when he worked as a volunteer for German-based Aid to the Church in Need in South and Central America with his friend, Tom Hoar.*

Tom and I were the first Britons to offer ourselves as volunteer labourers to the charity Aid to the Church in Need. We worked in five parishes over a period of seven months, with only our destinations worked out for us beforehand and one contact in Mexico.

We stayed with farmers and parish priests and were welcomed as charitable volunteers as well as guests sharing a common faith.

We were expecting to help build a chapel in Santa Cecilia, Chile, but were given the job of designing it from scratch, keeping within the budget provided by our charity. The community had been driven out of its former parish when the valley was flooded to form a reservoir. One local claimed: 'We don't need a police force. What we need is a church.'

Instead of flying to Panama City, Tom and I paid US$40 to ride in a wooden boat which was delivering 30 tons of beer along the Caribbean coast. We spent three days travelling with crazy Colombians, sleeping on top of crates of beer. We had to cross the border on foot, where we were fully searched.

In Panama City, we were stopped by a man claiming to be a policeman. He questioned us about how we had got into the country. We decided to get a room in a hotel. Later that night, we were woken by hammering on the door. We were terrified, but eventually opened the door.

It was the police. They tore our room apart, strip-searched us both, arrested us and put us in a cell for eight hours. There was no explanation, and no one could speak English. Eventually, we both paid $300 to be let out.

Adam and Tom bought an open-ended return ticket for one year for £730 from **STA Travel***. They flew to Santiago, Chile and returned from Mexico City, working in and travelling through Chile, Bolivia, Peru, Colombia, Panama, Honduras and Mexico.*

Al Siddons *was 19 when he went to Nepal, India and South-East Asia.*

I had jobs organised through contacts in Nepal and India before I set off on my travels, but as it turned out I need not have bothered. The highlights of my trip were when I found myself work.

I thought I had arranged a job through the Nepali Government Volunteer Organisation, working in Kathmandu Zoo. But when I arrived in Nepal I discovered they had never heard of me. I got the job anyway, but was upset by the treatment of the animals. There wasn't much for me to do. I was bored a lot of the time and left.

I found another job, teaching children English, through a Tibetan woman. I turned up at school at 8.30 the next morning to find I had to begin work right away. I hadn't done any TEFL training, but it didn't seem to matter.

My main achievement there was building a library from scratch and cataloguing 3,500 books, which had been donated by a US charity but had lain around for ages.

After trekking around the mountains of the Annapurna Circuit in Nepal for a month after Christmas, I made the

Charlie Wilcocks taught English in a school in Kathmandu

difficult journey to Ladakh. I had organised a job with the Ladakh Farm Project from Britain. I lived with a refugee family for a month, working on their subsistence farm, ploughing, weeding and herding donkeys. It was the best month of my life.

Although I had organised parts of my travels beforehand, by far the most rewarding parts were the spontaneous and unplanned adventures.

Al bought his flights in advance through **Trailfinders** *for £1,100.*

Charlie Wilcocks *was 18 when he organised a teaching position in Nepal through a schools project and then travelled through Asia.*

I decided I would like to teach children, and had heard that Nepal was beautiful. I decided to use a smaller company because the big ones charge huge amounts of money, thousands rather than hundreds, and to me the end result is more like a package deal than an independent travelling adventure.

I decided to find out about smaller companies and ended up paying a non-money-making organisation called ROAMA Schools Project a fraction of the GAP price for organising nothing but the essentials.

The ROAMA Schools Project deals specifically with teaching in Nepalese schools. A teaching position was arranged for me at a boarding school in Pokhara, Kathmandu. I taught children aged 9, 13 and 16 years. There was a huge variation in the standard of spoken English. Some of the children were excellent while others didn't have a clue, so I had to prepare different tasks. I taught them grammar, but mostly spoken English, using games such as hangman. I also got them to write short plays and read them aloud.

It was fairly easy to gain the children's respect through a mixture of smiles and firmness. I don't agree with the cane, but it was always there and used by the principal if anyone stepped out of line. I got to know the 15 boarding students well because I slept and ate with them. We played football in the evenings which proved a universal way of making friends.

I felt I made a mistake in buying a round-the-world ticket. It proved very restrictive and I often wanted to travel overland. Doing it again, I would buy one flight out, to a centre such as Bangkok or Hong Kong, and travel overland from there, taking money with me to buy flights when I needed to, especially since it is cheaper to book tickets in Asia than in the UK.

Charlie's round-the-world ticket cost £1,500 from **STA Travel***. His teaching position was arranged through* **ROAMA Schools Project** *for £250*

Hot tips

- Travel light
- Brave it alone: organisations are often expensive and restricting
- Take black underwear: it hides the dirt
- Use shoes broken in at least six weeks ago
- Keep a journal
- Take a stash of dollars (useful for bribery)
- Take a powerful torch
- Get the latest vaccination advice for your destination
- Check your insurance cover
- Get a hotmail address
- Don't fall in love

The Sunday Telegraph 15 August 1999
© Telegraph Group Limited 2000

Trouble free travel

It's that time of year when everyone is looking ahead to trips abroad and lots of sunshine. **Esther Cameron** of the National Youth Agency's youth information team gives young people a few practical tips for planning safer, more organised holidays.

Travelling safely

IF YOU ARE planning to be away from home for some time it may be useful to spend a bit of time thinking carefully about what to take with you. Here are a few suggestions for making a trip abroad a safe and organised one.

Clothing

- Don't take too much clothing – remember it will have to be carried around from one destination to another.
- Take clothes that will stand up to frequent washing!
- Take a long-sleeved shirt to protect skin against sunburn in the heat of the afternoon and mosquitoes in the evening.
- On an extended trip, it is useful to have something a bit smart in your luggage. It may help if you need to deal with officials.
- Remember that while you are on holiday and may wish to wear exactly what you want, others may not feel as comfortable about casual dress. In some countries appearance is very important, and that includes personal hygiene and grooming!
- If you are going to hot countries it is still worth taking a warm jumper or jacket. The evenings can be very cold and there will be some chilly days in the colder seasons.

Money

You need to be practical about how much money you've got, how long it will last and how you are going to carry it. If you take it all as cash and lose your wallet then you will be really stuck. Traveller's cheques are a better way of carrying money around – these can be collected before you go. Remember that the cheques should be signed before setting off otherwise it may be difficult to cash them.

Other useful items:

- A telephone charge card.
- Two photocopies of your passport, visas, insurance policy, air tickets, insurance policy and travellers cheques issuing receipts. You should keep one copy with them when you travel (separate from the originals), and leave one copy at home with someone you trust.
- Some spare passport photographs.
- A doctor's note for any medicine you may carry in case you are stopped at customs.

A useful guide is Mark Ashton's *Everything You Need to Know Before You Go: Information and Advice for Independent Travel* (ISBN 0952512815, price £2.99)

Safety advice for specific countries

Before travelling it may be useful to get background information on the countries you plan to visit from the Foreign and Commonwealth Office Travel Advice Unit. The unit gives advice to travellers about security and related matters – this is particularly useful in areas where there has been fighting, outbreaks of disease or natural disasters. The Consular Division of the Foreign and Commonwealth Office also produces leaflets containing dos and don'ts for major destinations.

Information about the Foreign and Commonwealth Office Travel Advice Unit is also available on BBC Ceefax page 470 onwards or on the internet.

Foreign and Commonwealth Office
Travel Advice Unit
FCO Travel Advice Unit
Tel: 020 7238 4503/4504 (9.30am to 4pm)
Fax: 020 7238 4545
Website: http://www.fco.gov.uk/

Help from the British embassy

If young British citizens get into trouble overseas they should contact a British consulate immediately. The main consulate in a country is part of the embassy or high commission in the capital city. There are often smaller consular offices, including honorary consulates, in other cities and towns. It may be wise for you to carry a list of British consular offices in the countries you plan to visit – the Foreign and Commonwealth Office produces leaflets with lists of addresses of British embassies, consulates, high commissions and consular offices in major world tourist destinations. If there is no British consulate you can seek help from a consulate of another country in the European Union.

Leave details of your route

It is a good idea for you to leave details of your proposed route with family or a friend, particularly if you are travelling from one country to another. It is advisable to keep in regular contact with someone if you are going on an extended trip.

Using a poste restante address

One of the great joys of travelling is arriving at a post office to find letters waiting from people back home! To arrange for letters to be sent to them, you should tell friends at home that you will be in a certain place by a certain date. Ask friends to send all mail to you c/o Poste Restante, General Post Office and then the city and country you are travelling to. Ask them to mark the envelope 'to await arrival' or 'to be called for'. It helps if the surname is written in bold capital letters.

The post office will keep mail in the poste restante section for a period of time (three months in the UK). You will be able to collect it as long as you can prove your identity with a passport.

Get online!

Another way of keeping in touch is to sign up with one of the free e-mail providers on the internet before leaving the UK. Hotmail, Yahoo and many others provide free e-mail services. Give your e-mail address to friends and family so they can keep you informed of the daily events back home. Cybercafes can now be found all over the world and it's a cheap and easy way to send regular news home.

The World Wise Directory

A new website has been developed by the Suzy Lamplugh Trust to help young people enjoy travelling around the world without getting into trouble. The World Wise Directory can be found at: http://www.brookes.ac.uk/worldwise

The site contains practical, country-specific tips to help young people get around safely, whether they are travelling on their own or with friends. There is also a book entitled *World Wise: Your Passport to Safer Travel* for those who do not have access to the internet.

Seasonal work abroad

There are a number of possibilities for seasonal work abroad. If you have language skills then your chances of better pay are improved. Opportunities include:

- **holiday company representative in resorts, camp sites, ski chalets**

This can be hard work and the pay is not always good. But there are advantages too – you get to stay in holiday locations, meet lots of other young people and can often make use of the facilities, such as swimming, water skiing, and sailing.

- **children's summer camp assistants**

Summer camps give you the opportunity to work on a children's camp – either directly with the children or related to the running of the camp, usually over the summer period. You get your flight paid for plus board and lodging and some pocket money with the opportunity to travel after the camp has finished. Camps can be privately run as a business or as a charity. One of the main schemes is called Camp America. Camp America runs annual recruitment fairs for the camps at venues in England and Scotland.

Camp America, Department EFL02, 37a Queens Gate, London SW7 5HR

- **agricultural work (such as grape picking)**

There is useful information about agricultural work in *Summer Jobs Abroad* published by Vacation Work (see below for the address and telephone). Agricultural work can be hard, back-breaking and poorly paid, but if you find the right place it can be a great opportunity to meet new people from another country, speak the language and get to experience rural life away from home.

For a comprehensive list of opportunities see *Summer Jobs Abroad, Working in Ski Resorts* and other publications by Vacation Work, 9 Park End Street, Oxford OX1 1HJ Tel: 01865 241978

Young People Now July 1999 (National Youth Agency)

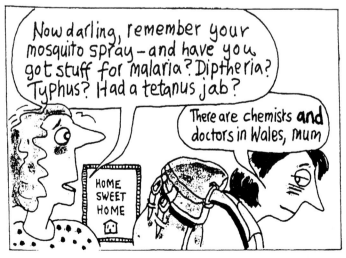

© Ros Asquith   *The Guardian 31 July 1999*

Travelling Light

Holiday kings need an extra plane for the knick-knacks

Spare a thought, as you squash in the tennis rackets, disco clothes and just-in-case items, for those doing the holiday packing for King Fahd of Saudi Arabia. He has taken not just a few extra sandals, beach towels and games in case he gets bored during his trip to Spain; he flew into Marbella with an entourage of 400 people and five extra Boeing-loads of luggage. And if you are worried that the shelf of thrillers you have lined up to read on the beach may cost you a bit in excess baggage charges, you may wonder what the 78-year-old monarch has decided to read that has pushed up his total luggage weight to 200,000 kilos.

The trouble is that after lugging the bulging suitcases to the airport, you still remember vital forgotten items: the hairdryer, the suntan cream, the diarrhoea pills. Or you may find that it is impossible to weave your way through a modern airport souk to the departure gate without impulse-buying loading you down with a couple of silk scarves, a nifty computer notebook and a bottle of rare malt Scotch. Saudi impulses are on a grander scale: at the last minute the King snapped up 200 mobile phones. Doesn't he realise that he can dial different numbers on them?

The palaver of a holiday is always worse if you have gaily invited friends and relations to drop in. In this case desert hospitality means stocking up to feed half the kingdom. The food bills at one Marbella shop come to £15,000 a day – not counting the largesse to be dispensed to servants, pilots, courtiers and a surgery of doctors standing by in the private hospital of the Mar-Mar palace complex. Local jewellers will not be the only ones counting their diamonds in anticipation of shopping expeditions by the King, or, more likely, his wives (always the big spenders on summer holidays).

The danger always of a trip abroad is that you will fall in love with the view. For most people this means returning next year. For the rich it means renting a villa; for the seriously rich, building one; and for King Fahd it means buying up half the seafront, erecting a pad on the hilltop that covers five football pitches, installing gold-plated lifts and then losing interest. For most holiday-home owners the bore is that you have to return each summer to get your money's worth. But a king's conscience is untroubled: this is Fahd's first visit for five years, and he is returning in style. But it will be costly. Most holidaymakers find that they need an extra bag for going home; the King will need a seventh Boeing just for the knick-knacks going back to Riyadh.

Editorial in *The Times 31 July 1999*
© Times Newspapers Ltd 1999

Travel sickness © Ros Asquith

SUCH a relief! Now we've got the new security alarm, we can go abroad with NO WORRIES!

The Guardian 3 July 1999

The 15.30 – London to Paris

'Ah, you need our one day super saver off-peak senior citizens cheap return budget shopper cut price awayday... oh you've just missed the train'

Prospect May 1999

Ever since childhood, when I lived within earshot of the Boston and Maine, I have seldom heard a train go by and not wished I was on it. Those whistles sing bewitchment: railways are irresistible bazaars, snaking along perfectly level no matter what the landscape, improving your mood with speed, and never upsetting your drink. The train can reassure you in awful places – a far cry from the anxious sweats of doom airplanes inspire, or the nauseating gas-sickness of the long-distance bus, or the paralysis that afflicts the car passenger. If a train is large and comfortable you don't even need a destination: a corner seat is enough, and you can be one of those travellers who stay in motion, straddling the tracks, and never arrive or feel they ought to – like that lucky man who lives on Italian Railways because he is retired and has a free pass.

Paul Theroux
The Great Railway Bazaar (1975)

NEXT EXCUSE
Signalling failure

The Oldie January 1999

Your train is delayed because the driver has the wrong sort of legs

Daily Mail Reporter

THE long and the short of it was that the rail commuters were going to be late again.

But what, the passengers wondered, would be the excuse this time?

It was a little late in the year for leaves on the line, and a little too early for the wrong kind of snow.

Would the reason be even more bizarre than a recent one of a yoghurt pot lid on a rail causing chaos?

The suspense was broken when the conductor wandered up and down the Northern Spirit train at Middlesbrough to explain that there would be a 15-minute delay because – the driver's legs were the wrong sort to overcome a technical problem that had arisen. Too short, to be exact.

Unlike his laughing passengers, the conductor managed to keep a straight face while he explained that the man in charge was only 5ft 1in and his swivel chair had broken, meaning he could not reach the pedals.

The commuters duly trooped off the Middlesbrough-Newcastle service and waited for its replacement to arrive – presumably with the swivel chair in full working order and the driver comfortably seated and able to operate the pedals.

Designer Tony Locke, 46, travels to Hartlepool every day and he said he thought it was the best excuse of all time.

'I've been commuting for 12 years and it's the most ridiculous thing I've ever heard.

'It's certainly more original than snow or leaves on the line or the other pathetic excuses regularly given.

'The guard wasn't joking either – he gave the same excuse to everyone in the carriage who asked and he did it with a straight face.

'It's all very bizarre but it's not like a dwarf was driving the train.

'All the passengers had a good laugh about it and we did get to our destination if just a little late.'

A spokesman for Northern Spirit refused to comment on whether the excuse was a tall story.

She added: 'We have no evidence to suggest there was a problem with the driver's seat but we will be investigating the unusual explanation that appears to have been given to customers.

'We regret there was a delay as a result of a need to replace a failed train which meant the train operated 15 minutes late.'

Daily Mail 3 December 1999

Wing and a prayer

Many travellers endure long journeys by road or sea to avoid taking a direct flight. Kay Holmes confronted her darkest fear on a course at Manchester Airport

My fear of flying really took off somewhere between Moscow and Kiev 10 years ago. The air hostess, who had just served her baffled customers beakers of what looked and tasted like diluted blood, then disappeared not quite far enough behind a curtain at the front of the plane wielding a large spanner. Grunting and struggling sounds accompanied the occasional glimpse of a sweaty elbow from behind the curtain.

Water leaking from the ceiling of the plane cabin, fantastic amounts of turbulence and yet more blood water compounded this anxiety on the subsequent flights to St Petersburg and back to Moscow. Somewhere in the middle of this, it occurred to me that jokes about Aeroflot were more than anti-communist propaganda.

Back in London and thoroughly shaken, I didn't get on a plane again for about five years. I've only done two flights since then, neither without trauma. My last flight – coming home from Venice – was delayed for about 45 minutes because of fog. I decided that this was a sure sign that the plane, the sky and everything in between were doomed and I tried to get my luggage back from the baffled Italian check-in official.

I caused quite a scene in Venice airport – crying, shouting, spilling coffee. I got to the point of trying to make my partner Stuart ring up Eurorail and get us home by train before I ran out of steam and calmed down somewhat with the help of the flying phobics' equivalent of an edifying text (*Taking the Fear out of Flying*, by Maurice Yaffé).

Stuart was remarkably stalwart throughout this and somewhat galled that when we finally got on the plane, I sat with hypnotised calm through turbulence on the way home, while he had been reduced to gibbering jumpiness by my histrionics.

Just the thought of getting onto an aeroplane is enough to make me literally shudder with dread. That moment when you are crammed knee to knee with hundreds of other people and the door closes and you can't get out. The utter conviction that it will be your plane that crashes. The zillion odd noises that presage doom. The impossibility of believing that you will survive the flight.

I've never flown for work because, to me, getting on to a plane means that I have to prepare to die and, since being turned down by the Marines, I've never had a job I'd die for. Or kill for, actually – but that's another story. This has meant years of long, tedious rail, boat and car journeys, an over-familiarity with France and, once, a spectacularly rough five-hour crossing from Jersey during which all I could see from the upper deck windows was choppy seas and vomiting Bergerac fans.

So it was with more horror than enthusiasm that I approached the day-long Aviatours Fear of Flying course at Manchester airport.

The experience began with an advertisement for flying –

Virgin trains. No air conditioning for the two and a half hour peak-hour journey between London and Manchester on one of the hottest days of July. By way of compensation, harassed buffet staff handed out warm tonic water. A more satisfying payback would be to have Richard Branson strapped to a seat of one of his trains and forced to travel back and forth all day, allowing passengers the satisfaction of giving his beard a thwap as they struggle to the loos.

At least the night before I thought I was going to die was a memorable one. I stayed at the coolly beautiful Malmaison Hotel. It is the way hotels "should" be. I thought I'd died and gone to heaven. But maybe that was just the turn my thoughts were taking.

The morning session of the course was impressive. British Airways captain Richard Poad and senior first officer Richard Parkinson took us through the principles of flight, the training of pilots and the construction of aeroplanes. Did you know that the wings are all one structure, rather than being stuck, Airfix kit fashion, onto the side of the fuselage? And that a plane can fly 160 miles (or half an hour) even if all its engines fail? And that although many planes have three or four engines, they can all fly on just one? Why, by the end of the morning I was wondering why they bothered with engines at all. Both men inspired confidence. They clearly loved flying and knew a lot about it and – most impressive of all – despite

> **CABIN PRESSURE:**
> A plane carrying passengers on a course to help them overcome their fear of flying had to make an emergency landing at Manchester airport when an oil leak caused the cabin to fill with smoke.
>
> *Manchester Evening News 3 March 2000*

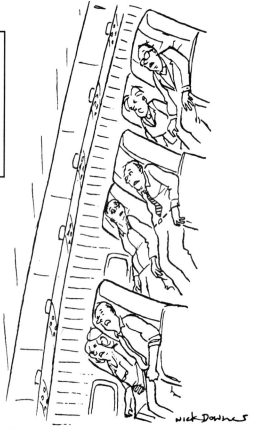

'Some ending to our fearless-flying course.'

The Spectator 1 January 2000

having an audience whose sheer anxiety would have dried Jerry Seinfeld, they managed to make us laugh. And not just at British Airways' tail designs.

During the coffee break we huddled in jumpy, sometimes tearful, little groups and exchanged flying stories. Barbara – a lovely woman from Liverpool – had once sailed back from Africa to avoid flying. It took two and a half weeks. Another, equally charming woman, had only flown once – 24 years ago on her honeymoon to Jersey. There was a wide range of ages, from a girl of about eight to pensioners and slightly more women than men. Some people had never flown (oh, how I envied them!) and others had either had nightmare flights or so many that they felt the odds were stacking up against them.

The pilots moved briskly through myths about flying. No, there is no such thing as a pocket of air you can just "drop" into. No, the "bings" of the cabin communication system are not a secret signal that we're all doomed. Gradually I felt Jeremy Paxman's apparent maxim for interviews – "Why is this lying bastard lying to me?" – becoming less helpful. Though I could have lived without the standard attacks on press reporting of air incidents – of course journalists get things wrong – but are we really expected to believe that airlines will voluntarily tell us the whole truth about their industry? I'm scared, not an idiot.

The afternoon session was somewhat less helpful. Although I think we all appreciated the deep breathing and relaxation techniques, the psychologist's approach was that our fear was based on an irrational perception of a perfectly safe situation. When someone made the quite reasonable point that in fact things do sometimes go wrong on flights and so some of the fear is rational, the psychologist's response was, "We have this thing we call a non-sequitur..." I believe that it was only our collective cold clammy dread which stopped us rising en masse and clipping the good doctor sharply around the ear.

And then to the flight. This was both the best and worst part of the day. We filed crocodile style through the airport to the terminal and check in and the departure lounge. At this point, many people, myself included, were visibly upset. I had thought this would make the flight more difficult, but, in fact, it was comforting to be among people with similar fears. If you see someone crying, you are more inclined to comfort them than think about your own anxiety. And a good deal of the encouragement on the course came from fellow phobics. One of our group got on the plane, then off, then on, then off again, finally deciding she really couldn't face it. This happens sometimes, apparently – though one out of 83 isn't a bad percentage – and often people who can't quite make the flight come back and succeed on a subsequent course.

The truly excellent thing about this day was that during the whole flight, from taxi-ing, through take off and at every strange noise or change in direction or adjustment in the wings, there was not only plenty of reassurance from the course helpers – skipping about the cabin looking delighted to be there – but also either Captain Poad or First Officer Parkinson's comforting voice over the intercom explaining exactly what was happening. They effectively narrated the flight for us, cutting off anxiety before it could really get a grip.

Although, as usual, I cried during take off and the ascent, that narration was precisely what I needed and helped a great deal. So much so that after a few minutes I was peering over the pilot's shoulder, out of the front of the cockpit window.

We flew from Manchester to well, frankly, Manchester for about an hour and the atmosphere on the plane was a heady cocktail of jubilation and raw fear.

We all cheered on landing, which is a difficult part of the flight for many people, though I have to say I'm dead keen on it and generally try to open the plane doors with my teeth as soon as the wheels hit the tarmac.

And as we poured out ashen faced and teary eyed into the arrivals hall, we made a strange contrast to the other tanned, bored looking travellers coming home from their holidays. Making that flight was a big step for many of us. For some it will be the start of a more relaxed approach to the ordeal; for others, confirmation that sea cruises are really the way to go.

As for me, triumphant, fearless, and with a Tufty Club-style "I've visited the flight deck" badge clutched in my sweaty palm, I decided never to fly again.

Only kidding.

Scaredy cats with no head for heights

Muhammad Ali was asked on television what he was most frightened of and replied:
"Flying. That's the only thing that terrifies me."

Isaac Asimov hated air travel and said: "I never fly, from sheer cowardice."

Dennis Bergkamp, the Arsenal striker, is afraid of flying. Some Arsenal fans believe this cost their team a Uefa Cup first-round tie in 1997. Bergkamp refused to fly to play in the away leg in Salonika, Greece. Arsenal lost the game 1-0 and could only draw the return match at Highbury 1-1

Science-fiction writer **Ray Bradbury** refuses to fly or drive a car: "I'm not afraid of flying – I'm just afraid of falling."

Ex-Olympic shot putter **Geoff Capes** went to the 1976 Montreal Olympics by land and sea rather than flying.

Actor **Tony Curtis** had it written into his contracts that he would not have to fly.

J Paul Getty refused to fly after a trip through several tornadoes in 1942.

Stuntman **Evel Knievel** used to drive across the USA, claiming he didn't want to give anyone an opportunity to kill him before he killed himself.

André Previn, who disliked flying, is reported to have told a stewardess during a particularly turbulent flight while Muzak was being played over the sound system: "Look, I don't care if there's only one chance in a million that we go down. I don't want to die to Lawrence Welk."

Ronald Reagan was convinced he "held the plane up in the air by sheer willpower."

Marge Simpson from the Simpsons had to visit a psychiatrist to help overcome her fear of flying when the family won a free trip to any state of their choice. (Homer is afraid of sock puppets.)

Mr T from the A-Team: "I pity the fool who thinks BA Baracus will fly in any plane!"

...also, allegedly, singers **Cher, Aretha Franklin** and **Michael Jackson**, band leader **Louis Prima** and **Glenda Jackson MP**

But no longer ...
Robert Smith, of The Cure, who used to insist on crossing the Atlantic by QE2. "I've lost my fear of flying, and heights also" he told *Rolling Stone*. "I think that it was really the fear of death that I couldn't get a grip on. I've lost the romantic notion that death is something to be respected, and brought myself to finally sort out the underlying fear. But my fear of spiders is still left over ..."

The Guardian 31 July 1999

TRAVELLERS CAUGHT UP IN THE NET

I am a Luddite. I am also a travel agent, and declare my interest lest I be accused of partiality. I am writing to save you all from the false friend, who, it is claimed, will free you from your chains. I am writing to save you from the Internet.

What has prompted me to write are those clients who have come unstuck with the microchip god they worship. The current belief is that what comes from computers will deliver precisely what the consumer wants: choice. But that choice is really just an illusion.

You must be aware that service providers, hotels and the like, are going to show themselves in the best possible light on the Net. That's OK, but it doesn't necessarily tell the whole truth. A hotel may offer lots of facilities but won't state what condition they are in. Is there a better hotel nearby which is not on the Net? You can only get such impartial advice from a travel agent.

And what about price? By cutting out the middleman, do you get a cheaper deal? Well, no. The hotel will sell at the rack (public) rate and just keep the agent's commission. If you book through a specialist agent you tend to get access to bulk deals or your travel agent's contract prices, which are often much cheaper than rack rates.

And airlines are no better. You may get a cheap ticket from the Net, but an airline is selling its own services. It doesn't tell you that another carrier is cheaper or has better stopover facilities or offers discounts on regional flights or on air passes.

What if something goes wrong when you're on holiday? Your travel agent's rep will be on hand if you have been sensible. But if you have booked it all yourself, defenestrating your VDU when you get back is the only satisfaction you are likely to get.

But why bother? The travel industry is now so well regulated that it seems incredible to me that anyone would voluntarily side-step the safeguards. By booking the loosest of packages you qualify for superb consumer protection under the Package Travel Regulations.

I am a microchip atheist. I preach heresy but you know I am right. So go on, change your anorak for a cardy and pop down to see your travel agent.

Andre de Mendonca

The writer is a director of the specialist travel company South American Experience

The Independent 18 September 1999

Buy before you fly

Is there no escape from the mall? asks poet **Alan Brownjohn**

ond Street Underground station has long been a commercial arcade; I remember finding an exit for a bewildered Bulgarian who thought he had been delivered into a shopping precinct, with no access to the outside world. This month I was, for the same reason, as perplexed as any foreigner when I went through Terminal 2 at Heathrow Airport for a flight to the Balkans.

At the ground floor check-in desks, things were the same as ever. The ticket formalities over, I made my way with hand-luggage and boarding pass to the escalator rising to the Arrivals and Departures hall. At the top, I wondered if I had missed a floor and emerged into a separate shopping annexe.

For as long as I could remember there had been a few shops and a café of sorts in this area, to which lately had been added stalls set up by encyclopaedia and mobile-phone salesmen. Now, in what should be a place designed to help arriving and departing travellers, there seemed to be shops and nothing else.

People wandered about, dazed by the displays and disconcerted by the lack of information and clear signs. The large boards providing flight data had gone. To know whether my flight was delayed or not, I had to squint at a small screen on a wall; not so comfortable for the short-sighted.

Inside, at the security x-rays and gateways, things seemed the same as ever. But after that you might as well have been at Brent Cross, or the Hatfield 'Galleria', or any other out-of-town complex. I wandered past the Duty Free regions, where I was solicited by persons trying to sell me Special Offer teddy bears and aftershave (I have a beard). With difficulty I recalled that I should be watching screens and listening to announcements.

But where were the screens? And when would they give you, on the public address system, that useful reminder that you were advised to go to Gate 17 *at once*? There were far fewer screens than before, spaced out much more widely and located by looking for groups of puzzled Italians or Japanese staring upwards, their backs turned on displays of socks or camcorders. The old insistent Tannoy was silent, and I began to feel that the airport must want you to stay here and buy and buy, regardless of your flight.

Eventually I somehow discovered that my 12.00 flight would leave one hour late, so I buried myself in my newspaper. Too deeply. All at once the screen was telling me, in small print, that it was just ten minutes to departure time. So where was the exit leading to the gates? Small, wholly inadequate signs pointed vaguely into a vista of even more cosmetics and confectionery emporia. Setting out up some stairs in one direction, I found it was the *wrong* direction. In despair I asked an assistant standing in front of a clothes store, 'Please, where are the aeroplanes?' She did not know, and seemed not to care.

At last I could see a familiar corridor with gate-numbers to right and left. At one stage (warning or apology?) a notice told me that there would be no more shops, bars or restaurants beyond that point. But there were – shops full of shining goods guarded by bored assistants, and mostly empty of customers.

Shops haven't yet penetrated the last lounges before the descent into the tunnel and onto the aircraft, where I arrived with all of a minute to spare. But I assume they will. At the final desk I said to the official checking boarding-passes, 'I nearly lost this flight. This has become about as confusing and unhelpful an airport as you'd find anywhere.' 'Quite right, sir,' he replied. 'Privately, we think so too. But you try telling anybody.'

On my return I wanted to tell somebody what a wretched insult of a place Terminal 2 at Heathrow has become for travellers who don't go there for a shopping spree. When I contacted the airport and described my problem, the operator said, 'Oh yes, it's certainly become a bit like that,' and passed me on to the terminal management. I listed my frustrations and told them, 'You'd think you were in a shopping mall.' 'But it *is* a shopping mall,' they told me. That was candid enough, but no real satisfaction. I pursued the matter of screens and signs, and it was acknowledged that things were not all they should be, and that 'the signage' was under review. While they are about it, reviewing 'the shoppage' as well might not be a bad idea.

The Oldie March 1999

BUDGET AIRLINES BAGGAGE

The Spectator 2 October 1999

The Evening Class

ARMCHAIR TRAVELLLING

If you could travel anywhere on a Friday evening — where would it be? A group of 15, from St Anne's in Lancashire, is taking off for Prague and still plans to make it home in time for tea. No Concorde or Tardis is involved. This is armchair travelling.

To be more accurate, it is hard-backed chair travelling. But this does not affect the passengers' spirits. Apart from two newcomers, everyone knows one another and there is a bubbling air of anticipation about the "virtual journey".

Tour guide is Gerry Mayers, a retired Customs officer who talks with infectious enthusiasm and prodigious knowledge. His research is meticulous — he can describe the geography and history of an area minutely and throw in a few well-chosen anecdotes for good measure. Finally, he shows a video to bring the place to life.

As with all good journeys, refreshments are provided. "Who's for wine?" asks Gerry like all attentive flight attendants.

The words of the Czech national anthem are passed around while the music is played on tape. Luckily for the travellers, no one is expected to stand up and sing.

Kathleen Klegg has travelled this way for eight years — and loves it. She has already visited Prague "in the flesh" but still finds that "this is a very interesting way to get to see these places . . . last week it was China."

Jean and Frank Wilson enjoy real holidays too, but admit "we are not very adventurous. So to come and find out about a place gives us more confidence".

After a break comes a quiz and travel news. Everybody hoots at the story of an unfortunate man who fatally misjudged the length of his bungee cord. "Everything is worth learning," says Barbara Whally, "Gerry convinces you that you want to go to see the place."

Next week they're off to Egypt. Except for the couple on holiday.

MARTIN CHILD

Times Educational Supplement 19 February 1999 © Times Supplements Ltd

Ham Khan

Journal of Silly 18

I'm too sexy for my car - but not for yours!

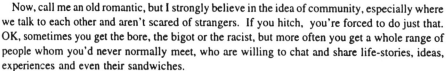

To those who've never tried it, and to those who claim to be too busy/rich/lazy to do it any more, hitch-hiking looks like a slow, dangerous and uncertain way of getting from A to B (possibly taking in C and D on the way).

However, in my experience, it is definitely the cheapest legal way to travel over long distances. It's more reliable and often faster than the train, and definitely faster than the coach; and it is basically green in that it encourages vehicle-sharing and has a negligible impact on the environment.

Now, call me an old romantic, but I strongly believe in the idea of community, especially where we talk to each other and aren't scared of strangers. If you hitch, you're forced to do just that. OK, sometimes you get the bore, the bigot or the racist, but more often you get a whole range of people whom you'd never normally meet, who are willing to chat and share life-stories, ideas, experiences and even their sandwiches.

To hitch successfully, it helps if you're relatively clean-looking, you stand in a good place to stop, you know how to get to your destination, and you're prepared for the odd half hour of breathing in fumes at some crappy motorway services.

So, if you ever want to travel (mostly) quickly and greenly, why not throw yourself on the mercy of the goodwill of a load of strangers? You never know, you might be surprised at how easy, cheap, quick, green and interesting it can be to travel in inherently antisocial and pollutant vehicles.

James Bowen, Huddersfield

Ethical Consumer April/May 1999

BEATING THE STRESS FACTOR

FLIGHT	STATUS
F6540	DELAYED
C7701	DELAYED
1545	10 HR WAIT
1625	15 HR WAIT
OOFF4	15 HR WAIT
161718	CANCELLED

Wesley Nike 2000

Planning ahead is the answer, say Dr Peter Barrett & Carole Cadwalladr

The risks associated with stressful or strenuous holidays – particularly in those with pre-existing disease – were laid bare by a recent Scottish study which revealed that of 952 Scots who died abroad, the commonest cause of death was cardiovascular disease. Only 4% died as a result of infection.

Even for those of us who are fit and well, stress can spoil what should be a restful and pleasant time. Despite the image of carefree relaxation, the reality is that travel is a very stressful business.

The key to reducing stress is to plan ahead. Think about the sort of holiday you will enjoy and if you are travelling with a partner or children, include them in the planning. There is nothing more annoying than being forced to go sightseeing

> *Lay out everything you think you will need and only allow yourself to pack half*

when all you want to do is relax on the beach. Try to agree beforehand how you will spend your time so that everybody is happy.

Consider a visit to your Travel Clinic a couple of months before you leave, particularly if you are going to an exotic destination. This will give your doctor or nurse time to sort out jabs or anti-malaria tablets. If you take regular medication, make sure that you have enough to last you through your trip and carry it in your hand luggage.

Ensure that travel documentation and passports are in order well before you go and invest in an insurance policy that includes the services of a medical assistance company with a 24 hour helpline. If you are unlucky enough to be ill while abroad, the company should be able to advise you and liaise with hospitals or doctors on your behalf. It is also worth finding out the contact details for the nearest British Embassy.

Do your packing early and don't take too much luggage. Hauling heavy cases around in hot weather is no fun. A sensible rule of thumb is to lay out everything you think you will need and only allow yourself to pack half. Ensure that your hand luggage contains a change of clothing suitable for your destination, together with a washing kit. If your luggage goes astray at least you can brush your teeth! And pack a jumper. Air-conditioning can make even Mediterranean airports chilly at night. If you have children include food, drink and toys in your hand luggage.

Plan your journey. If it is a long drive to the airport, it's worth considering booking a room in an airport hotel with parking facilities. You may actually save money by staying in such a hotel and taking advantage of a deal to leave your car there for two weeks for the price of a night's accommodation.

Allow plenty of time to check in and bear in mind that delays do happen, so take something to read or something for children to play with. Even if the airline knows your flight will be delayed, it will still want to have you at the airport in case an alternative is found. Arriving at the airport late and having to rush exacerbates what is already a tense situation.

British Airways and all other big carriers let you check in at Paddington before catching the Heathrow Express, and BA also have check-in facilities at Victoria for those using the Gatwick Express. Several charter airlines allow you to pay to use an airport lounge and have priority check-in.

For £15 Britannia (0870 607 6757) will give you access to the lounges at Gatwick, Manchester, Stansted and East Midlands airports. And for £35 you can check in at a priority desk and take 10kg extra luggage. Airtours (0870 608 1940) operates a similar scheme for £29.

Check if there are any delays before going through to departures. There is no way back out again. At some airports – Dalaman in Turkey, for example – the air-side facilities can get extremely congested if there are several delayed flights.

And make sure you have some foreign currency. It is nerve-racking to be stranded in an airport without the wherewithal to buy supplies.

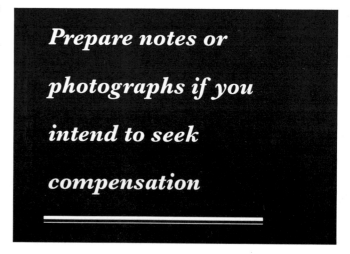

> *Prepare notes or photographs if you intend to seek compensation*

Finally, at your destination, if things are not to your liking, don't get angry. Take a deep breath and explain calmly what the problem is and how you wish it to be resolved. If that fails then determine to make the best of it but prepare notes or photographs if you intend to seek compensation.

The Daily Telegraph 31 July 1999
©Telegraph Group Limited 2000

Slapping on sunscreen is not enough, say health experts. We must rethink our beach habits

Summer's burning issue

Sunscreens alone are failing to protect thousands of holidaymakers from severe sunburn, skin experts warned this week.

A survey published by the Department of Health shows that a quarter of men and a fifth of women are sunburnt at least once a year.

The dangers were highlighted this week by the case of nine-year-old Luke Ford from Falkirk, Scotland, who was taken to hospital, with severe burns after spending last weekend – the hottest of the year – on Brighton beach. He was wearing a factor 25 sunscreen, and wore a shirt and hat on the first day.

His mother, Dawn Ford, said the sunscreen, Boots Soltan, had been reapplied throughout the day. 'Obviously, that wasn't enough because on the night of the second day his back and arms were covered in blisters the size of golf balls.'

Luke was bandaged, given skin cream and made to drink two litres of water. He also had sunstroke. 'They told me that the top layer of his skin was completely burned off,' Mrs Ford said. 'They said he now has a higher chance of developing malignant melanoma. We were told he should use factor 40 and wear a hat and shirt because he's so white.'

Brian Diffey, professor of photobiology at Newcastle General Hospital, said the problem lay in the way

people use sunscreens. 'Most people do not use nearly enough sunscreen,' he said. 'All manufacturers test sunscreens to an agreed thickness, which is 2 milligrams per square centimetre of skin. In practice people don't apply this amount because if they did then a typical adult would need to apply something like a third of a bottle per application.

Holiday Hell: Luke Ford's burns   *Photo: Rosemary Behan*

Typically, people apply 0.5mg to 1mg per square centimetre. That means that if you use an SPF 15 in the typical way you are probably going to get an SPF of only five on your skin.'

His back and arms were covered in blisters the size of golf balls

Prof Diffey said that as well as not using enough sunscreen, people were not applying it properly. 'Most people put it on patchily, leaving some areas completely unprotected. They also tend to rub it into the skin which means it can't form a barrier.

If the sunscreen penetrates into the skin, it goes past the layers of the skin cells where the sunburn reaction starts to form.'

A spokesman for Boots said that all its packaging contains application advice stating that sun lotion should be 'applied liberally' 15 minutes before going into the sun and then reapplied every one to two hours and after swimming. 'All our products are tested using standard methods to ensure the correct level of sun protection,' he added.

A spokesman for the Department of Health, which issues guidelines on sun safety, said it is considering instructing manufacturers to say how many applications a bottle of sunscreen contains. 'At the moment, we advise people not to rely on sunscreen alone but to wear loose-fitting clothing, even in

Children should not be on the beach between 11am and 3pm

Britain.' The Department of Health survey showed that people were less likely to use a sunscreen when sunbathing in Britain, but sunbathing was the primary cause of skin cancer. There are 40,000 new cases of skin cancer diagnosed each year in Britain, and 2,000 people die of the disease.

A combination of protection methods is necessary to protect children, according to the Health Education Authority. Sunscreen should be applied so that it can still be seen on the surface of the skin, and all children should be made to wear hats and shirts and kept out of the sun when it is at its hottest, said a spokeswoman. 'But still thousands of people are burned unnecessarily because they don't use a combination of methods,' she said.

Dr Julia Newton-Bishop, a consultant dermatologist for the Imperial Cancer Research Fund, said that people needed to 'completely reorganise their holidays' to prevent sunburn.

'Children should not be on the beach between 11am and 3pm,' she advised. 'I was in Cornwall last week and there was a lot of burnt skin about.

'Parents must teach by example and show that it's reasonable to have a beach holiday and come back the same colour as you went.'

Rosemary Behan

The Daily Telegraph 31 July 1999
© Telegraph Group Limited 2000

The Spectator 28 August 1999

'A perpetual holiday is a good working definition of hell.'

George Bernard Shaw

Prospect March 1999

HOLIDAY DISASTER

Fiona Bacon arrived in Santiago four days late, thin, miserable and starving

"WOULD PASSENGER Fiona Bacon, travelling to Santiago, please make herself known at the flight desk?" Deceptively good news awaited me; the airline had overbooked my flight – would I be prepared to switch to another slightly later, in return for an upgrade? I called my boyfriend in Chile and accepted the offer, looking forward to a better class of bench in the business class lounge. Stuffed full of dry roasted peanuts and Bloody Marys, I arrived at my newly designated gate. I was alarmed to find that the flight would be stopping twice en route – at Aruba and Guayaquil – but the wide seats and lavish toilet bags in business class quelled my fears.

At breezy, palm-strewn Aruba, the plane landed for re-fuelling, and we trooped off to the spacious Portakabin of a terminal. After several hours' wait, everyone was becoming irate. A formidable stewardess was despatched to pacify us with refreshment vouchers, and 300 people stampeded for one hastily opened hot-dog stand. After that came the announcement that we would be detained in Aruba for a further 24 hours because a new part for the 747 aircraft had to be flown in from Europe. Without luggage, we were all driven through the pearly dawn to cheap hotels, with no air-conditioning, some distance from the beach.

The sheen had fully worn off business class as I took my place again, wearing the same clothes I had set out in. Next stop, Ecuador's Guayaquil airport terminal, resting in what looked like a shallow bomb crater, was staffed by gun-toting militia, and had the welcoming appeal of an abattoir. Eight of us had been upgraded, and we'd been assured that airline reps would greet us on the ground. After some hours wandering around in sweltering 80 per cent humidity, completely abandoned, we were forced to jump over barriers and hammer on the airline's office doors.

Sensing impending violence, they sent out a visibly pregnant rep to deal with us. She gave us all $250 worth of miscellaneous cash orders (MCOs) – valid only for further flights, not much-needed beers – and told us that, since there was no connecting flight to Santiago that day, we would be spending a night in Guayaquil at the Hotel Colon. Another night, another toilet bag, but still no sight of our luggage. We were told too that we'd have to give back our MCOs. I went to my room and wept buckets.

Meanwhile, in Santiago, my boyfriend was going mad with worry – no one from the airline had been able to tell him where I was. With just five minutes' free phone time, I couldn't get through. Next day the airline reps left us at the mercy of customs staff. "Why are you spending only one day in Guayaquil? What's inside all these toilet bags?" I was singled out for special treatment, my luggage decanted on to the runway and every embarrassing item pored over in detail. Finally, I arrived in Santiago four days late, thin, exhausted, and feeling like a refugee, albeit one with an unparalleled collection of travel toothbrushes.

The Independent on Sunday
17 January 1999

'Why has not this man been buried?'

About to leave for Africa in 1893 Mary Kingsley is alarmed by a phrasebook for Dahomey

It was the beginning of August 1893 when I first left England for 'the Coast'. Preparations of quinine with postage partially paid arrived up to the last moment, and a friend hastily sent two newspaper clippings, one entitled 'A Week in the Palm-oil Tub', which was supposed to describe the sort of accommodation, companions, and fauna likely to be met with on a steamer going to West Africa, and on which I was to spend seven to *The Graphic* contributor's one; the other from *The Daily Telegraph*, reviewing a French book of 'Phrases in Common Use' in Dahomey. The opening sentence in the latter was, 'Help, I am drowning.' Then came the inquiry, 'If the man is not a thief?' and then another cry, 'The boat is upset.' 'Get up, you lazy scamps.' is the next exclamation, followed almost immediately by the question, 'Why has not this man been buried?' 'It is fetish that has killed him, and he must lie here exposed with nothing on him until only the bones remain,' is the cheerful answer. This sounded discouraging to a person whose occupation would necessitate going about considerably in boats, and whose fixed desire was to study fetish.

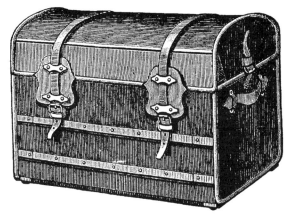

So with a feeling of foreboding gloom I left London for Liverpool – none the more cheerful for the matter-of-fact manner in which the steamboat agents had informed me that they did not issue return tickets by the West African lines of steamers.

Mary Kingsley, Travels in West Africa (1897)

Stars wane for the Fawlty hoteliers

The game is up for hotels that are beyond a joke, reports **Valerie Elliott**

THE days when seaside hotel landladies offered tiny rooms with a double bed pushed against the wall are about to disappear.

In future any hotel wishing to qualify for a star ranking from the AA, the RAC or the English Tourist Board must follow strict rules on bedtime. The efforts are part of a strategy to improve tourism standards and put an end to hotels that are run in the manner of *Fawlty Towers*.

More than 100 hotel inspectors have been told that in future double beds in star-ranked hotels must have access from both sides. Beds must also now come in standard sizes — a double must measure 6ft 4in by 4ft 6in, while a single bed must be 6ft 3in by 3ft.

Four-star hotels, however, must offer a choice of larger bed sizes, including queen and king-size beds, and four-posters. Even a one-star hotel must offer a modern bed with a secure headboard.

As for clean sheets, a guest at a one-star can expect a change every four days, every three days at a three-star, every two days at a four-star and every day at a five-star hotel.

There are also new cleaning standards for every grade of hotel, particularly for bathrooms.

A spokesman for the English Tourist Board said: "We

also expect all flat surfaces to be free of dirt, dust, grease or marks. We are trying to eradicate all those greasy surfaces; we want them to be clean and glistening and we don't want any broken glasses. We want rooms to be checked thoroughly before they are let."

The minimum requirement by July 1 for a one-star hotel is six letting bedrooms, of which 75 per cent should have en-suite or private bathrooms. Each room must have its own heating control and guests must also have use of a restaurant, lounge and residents' bar.

The minimum set breakfast menu for a one-star hotel will be fruit juice and cereals, bacon and eggs, coffee, tea and toast, or a regional offering. All hot food should be "well-cooked and presented grease-free and served at the correct temperature. Care should be taken to ensure that the juices are chilled and that the toast is crisp, not limp, and that coffee is freshly made."

A three-star hotel would offer the same plus a good range of hot and cold food and a selection of good-quality jams, marmalade, ground and decaffeinated coffee, and choice of tea.

A five-star breakfast must also offer freshly squeezed fruit juices and fresh fruit, cold meats, cheeses, croissants and pastries and food for special diets such as diabetic jams.

In England there are 6,458 hotels of which 2,869 are subject to inspection by the ETB, AA or RAC, while of the 26,946 guesthouse accommodation premises, 9,149 are subject to inspection.

The Government is determined that there should be changes and that tourists should no longer be confused by the present grading systems, which offer stars, crowns, rosettes, ticks or even keys to show the different standards of quality. Some perfect hotels cannot get even "highly commended" because there are no hospitality trays in the bedroom.

The new scheme, developed by the ETB with the AA and the RAC, will offer a single grading system of between one and five stars for hotels and a diamond quality mark — again graded between one and five — for guesthouses, small pubs and bed-and-breakfast rooms. The system is also expected to be taken up in Wales, Scotland and Northern Ireland.

Inspectors have already started checking standards and the new symbols could be on display at some premises before the summer.

But Chris Smith, the Culture Secretary, gave warning yesterday that if the new rating system could not be made to work he would impose stringent national standards on hotels and guesthouses.

The Times 27 February 1999 © *Times Newspapers Ltd 1999*

Budget Hotels Recommended

People who stay in budget hotels are more likely to recommend them than those staying at any other type of hotel. Scher International, which rates hotel services, said yesterday 93 percent of those staying in a budget hotel would recommend it versus 88 percent in five star hotels, 82 percent in four star hotels and 73 percent in three star establishments. Budget hotels also beat five star hotels in speed of check-in. Five star hotels fared best in meeting guests' needs and in putting things right then they went wrong.

Scheherazade Daneshkhu

Financial Times 14 August 1999

Bright idea

I am writing this letter with great difficulty. I can hardly see what I am doing because the lighting in my hotel room in Brunei consists of four 20-watt bulbs. There is nothing wrong with my eyesight but I do find that hotel rooms and especially the writing desks are usually appallingly lit. In this hotel room, the light in my wardrobe has a higher wattage but I find working in there somewhat claustrophobic. Perhaps *Business Traveller*'s annual Reader Poll should include a question on the topic.

And where is the switch for the writing desk light? No, it's not at the desk; it's three metres away on a bedside console, which prompts the question: do the designers of hotel rooms ever stay in them?

The bumph in the room says that this hotel group has more than 400 hotels worldwide and that it meets the needs of today's busy traveller. If they think 20-watt bulbs meet my needs, then I suggest they change all the bulbs at corporate headquarters to see if that meets their needs.

K Hewitt, Macclesfield, UK

Business Traveller February 2000

Hotel Notices

— note —

'Please do not bring solicitors into your room.'
Room notice, Chiang-Mai, Thailand

— note —

'Please leave your values at the front desk.'
Hotel lift, Paris

'This hotel is renowned for its peace and solitude. In fact, crowds from all over the world flock here to enjoy its solitude.'
An Italian hotel brochure

SOOTHING DUMMY

Staff at a new hotel near Perth, Scotland, have been provided with a shop-window dummy on which to vent their anger, rather than on guests.

The Herald 14 July 1999

'It's the business of hotels to be one step behind the times – hotels, like colonies, keeping up a way of life that is already outmoded.'
Alan Bennett

'The great advantage of a hotel is that it's a refuge from home life.'
George Bernard Shaw

A day in the life of a lifeguard

They're our very own Baywatch babes, bringing a touch of glamour as well as safety to the UK's coastline. When Wendy, 37, is not in her smart office outfit as an Administration Manager, you'll find her and her team of lifeguards in swimsuits, patrolling the beaches of Bournemouth. Although Wendy, who is currently single, is adept at handling emergencies in and out of the water, most of her time is spent trying to stop people getting into trouble in the first place. Here she tells AMANDA DRIVER about her work...

Because of the Baywatch programme, lifeguards have a much sexier image. I often get wolf-whistles and cheeky comments. Guys walk past our unit and shout, "Where's Pamela?" We just respond with a smile and stick our chests out.

Sometimes people use our service for the most bizarre reasons. Last Sunday morning a man started frantically waving from the pier. We shot over there with a horrible feeling that there would be a body in the sea. When we reached him he kept pointing in the water but I couldn't see anything. It turned out that the lady on the pier who did the tarot had dropped one of her cards.

Once you're a lifeguard it's hard to switch off. I find myself keeping an eye out even when I go swimming at a pool.

When I was 18 on holiday in Barbados with my sister, we were having a quiet drink in the bar when a family got straight into the pool with their young son. I looked over my sister's shoulder and realised the boy was in trouble. I jumped in and pulled him out. His parents had no idea he was drowning. I did suggest they got him a pair of armbands.

The public are usually very helpful when it comes to a situation such as a missing child. But sometimes they ignore the warning flags because the sea doesn't always look as dangerous as it actually is.

About ten years ago, on a hot Bank Holiday Monday, a member of the public alerted us to a young woman who had got stuck on one of the groynes.

The groynes go out about 50 metres from the beach. They're covered in slime and barnacles, and where she had tried to cling on her swimsuit had been ripped to shreds and her body was covered in grazes. We managed to pull her out and get her to hospital. Luckily, she made a full recovery.

We posted a lifeguard on each groyne to try and stop people going near them, but people kept piling into the sea, even though the red flag was up. I think people thought, "It won't happen to me". Unfortunately, it did and we rescued 86 that one afternoon.

Another problem

Photo: Phil Yeomans

'We raced to a man waving frantically to us from the pier. The tarot lady had dropped one of her cards into the sea.'

is the marker buoys. They're like magnets to people who swim toward them without realising how far out they are. We have had a lot of incidences where we have to go out and bring people back in.

When I'm not working I go surfing in North Devon or Cornwall, although I'm a better swimmer than surfer. My own board is 7ft 6ins long and called "Bill". We've had a lot of fun together.

I've always been a competitive swimmer. At school, I participated in the national schoolgirl championships and reached fifth place. When I was 14 I joined the Thames Rescue lifesaving club to get my bronze medallion. From the moment I joined I was in the competition team and competed at national level. When I moved to Hounslow School of Lifesaving I became national champion with the club.

My whole family is into swimming. At one point we all held a lifeguard qualification. My sister Jill is a lifeguard at Poole.

I moved to Bournemouth ten years ago. There are a few permanent paid lifeguards, but most of us work on a voluntary basis. I work every weekend and train a few times a week, either at the beach or in the local pool. We do all our own fundraising and keep the service afloat through our own efforts.

To be a lifeguard at the beach you need to hold the National Beach Lifeguard qualification. You have to re-qualify every two years. This involves having excellent fitness, resuscitation and first-aid skills. We also have to complete mock lifesaving rescues so that we're ready for a real emergency. A lot of the work that we do is first aid.

Being part of a lifesaving team has become a way of life to me. I've been well and truly bitten by the bug. It provides me with a great social life. After working we all have a drink together and, English weather permitting, the summer sees a lot of barbecues on the beach.

Last week, we had 26 volunteer lifeguards on duty, with ages ranging from 14 to 60. That's an inspiration to me and as long as I'm fit and healthy, I'm going to carry on doing what I love most.

The Mirror 14 August 1999

The Seaside Landlady

What's the attraction of being a seaside landlady? I'm never bored, I'm my own boss and you meet so many different people. My husband had always wanted to run a small hotel and I fell in with the idea when we came out of the Army. We had absolutely no experience and only one practice weekend when 16 of my sister's family and friends came to stay.

Why Blackpool? We went to Skegness first but a hotelier warned us off it. He told us it was a long, lean winter and the place to go was Blackpool. When we first came to look at properties during the Illuminations in October, the place was packed – you could hardly move on the prom. There were more people in Blackpool in October than there were in Skegness in July.

Do holidaymakers still expect the archetypal landlady? Yes. There are two types of landlady: the 'pinny' one who answers the door in her apron and slippers, and the glamorous, Bet Lynch type with big hair and lots of make-up. Then there's me! I wear smart casual and I'm a bit more trendy when we've got youngsters in.

How do you organise your day? I get up at seven and I'm lucky to have finished by nine at night. I do the cooking – breakfast between 8.30 and 9 and evening meal at five o'clock. I also clean the rooms – I've got a thing about shiny mirrors and taps – and shop for meat and fresh vegetables. In between, guests are arriving. Then I cook an evening meal for the four of us before I sit down in front of the television with the paperwork. That's when the phone starts ringing with bookings.

Who are the best guests? Old people are great – it's often like having your mum and dad to stay. They're not fussy about en suite and 99.9 per cent of them will eat anything. It is true that some people arrive as guests and leave as friends. We get around 300 Christmas cards from guests and lots of them say if you're in Fife, or Stoke-on-Trent, or wherever, just drop in. One old guy rings at Christmas and Easter to see how we are and again just before he

Kim Asplin

44, runs the Wynnstay hotel in Blackpool with her husband, Colin. The couple, who both left the Army seven years ago, share the house with their children Andrew, 20, and Natalie, 17, and up to 20 guests. They make more than £40,000 a year

comes to stay, because he's getting excited. He brings me chocolates.

And the worst? We have made mistakes with groups of young boys or girls, who are their own worst enemies. They come here and it's fun-time, Las Vegas on their doorstep. The men will get up in the night and they're so drunk, they'll pee in the room. And one guy left the bed soaked because his mate woke him up with a jug of cold water. Girls can be untidy, dirty beggars, they'll step out of their knickers and leave them on the floor and there'll be a pair of tights slung over the bathroom door.

Where do you go for your holidays? Tenerife, between November and Easter when we are closed, and we've been skiing to Austria.

What's it like being with your husband 24 hours a day? Not easy at first after spending long periods apart in the Army. We snap at each other more than ever now, but we've learned to argue in a whisper if there are guests around.
By Lynne Greenwood

Telegraph Magazine
7 August 1999
© Telegraph Group
Ltd 2000

'All work and low pay!'

Working conditions in the tourism industry make dire holiday reading, says Sue Wheat

As tourists, we are now well-armed with information from Watchdog-type programmes teaching us how not to fall prey to unscrupulous holiday companies. But no one, it seems, is giving a second thought to those working in the tourism industry.

This is as true in British tourist destinations as those further afield. In Manchester, a Blue Badge Guide lamented that, despite extensive local knowledge, his hard-earned guiding qualification, and the marketing push that the city is giving to tourism, few tourists want to pay more than a nominal fee for his services. Making a proper living through the profession is, for him, an impossibility.

And in London, a look behind the scenes into almost any hotel kitchen will reveal a legion of hard working overseas students and refugees.

The combination of long and unsociable hours, low pay, hard work and seasonal, temporary contracts is something only the young and those on the margins of society are willing to put up with.

Research by the Commission for Racial Equality shows that in the UK, 2% of white men work in the hotel and catering industry compared with 10% of black men, of whom almost all are in unskilled jobs. Full-time, manual, hotel and catering jobs paid £225.80 to men and a mere £170.80 a week to women last year - significantly lower than the national average wages for manual workers of £328 and £211 respectively.

Steve Pryle, Campaigns Officer for Britain's biggest union, the GMB, describes it as an Upstairs, Downstairs scenario. 'There are the few very well paid executives, and then most leisure and tourism workers exist on very meagre wages,' he says.

Pay and labour conditions are understandably worse in poorer destinations, with young workers in Third World countries often moving from rural areas into tourist destinations for work, convinced that the industry is glamorous and well-paying. What they invariably find are jobs as waitresses, cleaners and sales people, with hours and conditions that often make for a miserable existence.

And in Egypt, before you reach the sparkling, white tourist complexes that now make up Sharm El-Sheikh on the Sinai coast, you might notice a string of ugly, breeze-block buildings set back from the road. This is housing for the thousands of migrants that have flooded to the area in recent years. After building, cleaning or servicing luxury tourist accommodation owned by international hotel chains, the workers return to houses with the most basic of facilities and sleep six to a room.

Although monitoring workers' hours and conditions is not a common holiday pastime, on Thailand's Koh Samui island, I realised that the waitresses at our guest house were

working seven days a week, going to bed in the early hours when the last partygoers stopped drinking and getting up a few hours later to serve more sober guests breakfast. Shifts didn't seem to exist, time off was rare and they earned £1 a day. The guests had thought they were sullen and rude. In fact, they were exhausted.

Yet tourism is heralded as one of the key industries of the next millennium. The World Travel and Tourism Council estimates the industry will represent around $167 billion of the UK's GDP this year, which is almost 12.3% of our total economic activity, and that it will employ around 3.4 million people. It also estimates that, worldwide, travel and tourism supports around 200 million jobs directly and indirectly.

Tourism is an employment option more and more people and governments are turning to. But whether it will bring economic prosperity and security to most of the workers is questionable. Things may improve for workers in the UK through the minimum wage and the new Employment Relations Act which was given royal assent last month.

'Employers are now realising they can't ride roughshod over their employees,' says GMB's Steve Pryle. 'We will hopefully see an end to the hire-and-fire culture which has been very prevalent in these sectors. It will also help workers in the tourism and leisure industry become unionised and fight for better pay and treatment.'

Prospects for workers in tourism in less developed countries are not so bright. The Thai waitresses I met have little means of fighting for their right to sleep or be paid a reasonable wage.

Tourism may be a fundamental part of the global economy, but if Watchdog did a programme on how tourism workers fare, it would probably be outraged. Behind every holidaymaker's dream holiday are numerous workers worrying how to make ends meet.

The Guardian 14 August 1999

A PASSPORT to your new career

Temping is a good way to earn cash while you travel. But cross those borders with care.

If you're looking for a job that involves travel, don't be surprised if a recruitment agency recommends secretarial work. Not only is computer technology making secretarial work similar the world over, but it is also far more lucrative than the usual travel jobs such as nannying or bar work. In addition, it's fairly simple to get short or long-term placements and it's becoming easier to secure work before you've left Britain.

The recruitment consultancy Angela Mortimer plc is one of many British companies that has begun to team up with other consultancies around the world to set up exchange programmes.

'We realised that the quality of our interviewing techniques and the kind of secretaries we are after is almost identical to a recruitment agency in Sydney," explains director Amanda Fone.

'So we have set up a system in which we take on secretaries who that company has employed and who are looking to work in London – and they do the same for us." In fact, says Ms Fone, if you've done some work for Angela Mortimer and you tell them you're off to Australia at the weekend, there's every chance they could have a placement ready for you the following week.

Similarly, secretaries with the travel bug can take advantage of the larger recruitment consultancies which are setting up offices abroad. 'We have 3,000 offices across 52 countries," says Angela Lewis, resource manager at Adecco. 'For instance, we've just opened one in Japan. All applicants have to do is approach any Adecco office for our worldwide guide and then telephone the head office in the country they're interested in to arrange to have an application form mailed to them and to ask any questions they may have.'

Among these questions should be queries about whether it is legal for British people to work in the country in question. If yes, what documentation will you need and what financial arrangements do you need to make? How much can you expect to get paid and taxed? Australia is the current hot-spot for travelling secretaries, and provided you have a work visa, it is legal

to work for three months at a stretch. In other countries, however, doing anything other than voluntary work may not be allowed.

One way of getting round this, however, is to structure your trip according to where you can work. You could, for instance, spend time in South America and Canada where it is possible to find well-paid temping work before using your earnings to travel round the US, where it is illegal to work.

One advantage of using consultancies to get work abroad is that secretaries can work for them here while they save for their trip. 'It also enables them to add to their experience so that they can get a better job when they arrive at their destination,' adds Ms Lewis. 'In addition, they can build up their reputation. If a consultancy knows one particular secretary is reliable, they'll be far more likely to recommend them to other offices around the world.'

So what type of people apply? 'They tend to be young and female – often taking a year off between A-levels and university,' says Ms Lewis. 'But since the status and rates of pay of secretarial work have risen, there have been far more men and older people interested as well.'

One of the main concerns for travelling secretaries is what kind of language skills they'll need. This entirely depends on the consultancy

and country in question, the size of the company and your position within it, and the sector. Finance and banking, fashion and cosmetics and management consultancy, for example, are most likely to require some knowledge of the local language. But even if you find work in a foreign-speaking country that doesn't require you to know the language, it is worth attempting to learn the basics. Not only is it polite but it will improve your social life no end.

'Increasingly, managers are taking their foreign-speaking assistants with them on business travel, so learning a language could become a secretary's passport to travelling without even having to leave your current job,' points out Philippe Milloux, deputy head of the French Institute in London.

But knowledge of the language shouldn't be your only consideration when it comes to communicating as a secretary abroad. Understanding different business cultures is equally important. On shaking hands at the end of a negotiation with a German or French person, for example, you might congratulate yourself on having reached a deal. But in their eyes, the handshake may be no more than a polite leave-taking. Even apparently universal gestures such as nodding or shaking your head can lead to confusion. In Bulgaria and parts of Greece, Turkey and Iran, for example, 'yes' is signalled by a lateral head sway easily confused with the head shake.

'Get it wrong and you may not just confuse, but deeply offend overseas colleagues,' explains Angelena Boden, author of *The Cultural Gaffes Pocketbook* (£6.99, Management Pocketbooks). For instance, making a circle with your thumb and forefinger means 'OK' to an American or Briton, 'money' to a Japanese, and 'zero' to someone from the South of France. In Malta it means a male homosexual and in Greece it is an insult.

The solution, says Ms Boden, is to research every stage of your trip. Buy guidebooks about the country; study the *Lonely Planet* website (www.lonelyplanet.com); and ask recruitment consultancies what guidance they can offer you.

Kate Hilpern

The Independent 20 October 1999

Someone's got to do it
JOBS IN THE TRAVEL INDUSTRY

DAVID ABRAM is the author of several 'Rough Guide' books to India. He says the job leaves him needing a holiday to recover.

What do you love about your job?
At the beginning, it was tremendously exciting knowing that my opinions and experiences would end up in print. Also, researching a book forced me to explore off the beaten track, wander down alleys I wouldn't normally wander down, and generally find places I might not otherwise visit if I were on holiday. What most people don't realise, though, is that I spend maybe a quarter of my time travelling, and the rest researching and writing.

So what are the drawbacks?
It can get really lonely sometimes. I can be travelling for three or four months on my own, and you have to cover so much ground in that time that you don't have the opportunity to hang around and forge relationships. Every time I get back, I say to myself 'never again' – and that's before the writing starts. The next eight or nine months can be a pretty intense experience and I spend days in my pyjamas, putting the work off.

Doesn't it feel like you're on holiday?
When you're abroad, it's the opposite to a holiday: you get up early in the morning, and don't stop all day. Everything you see and feel may filter into the book. If you don't note everything down at the

time, you'll probably never get another chance. So, it's enjoyable but exhausting and it's easy to get run down or ill. I always have two or three weeks off when I get back.

Do you try to remain 'undercover' as much as possible?
Yes, but it's not always possible. I've done several books on Goa, so I'm pretty well known there. I try not to tell restaurants so that I don't get preferential treatment but being known can sometimes be advantageous; having a chat with the hoteliers can give me the sort of local details that make a guide seem less like it's written by someone passing through.

Do you ever get offered bribes in exchange for a mention in the guide?
A glowing guidebook entry can make all the difference

for a business so you get a lot of people asking to be included. We'll send someone to check it out, but that's about as far as it goes. The bottom line is, you've got to be dependable or your book – and the series as a whole – is going to suffer.

Is there a danger that travellers treat guidebooks as their bible, and the places that are mentioned become ruined?
It certainly happens, though it's difficult to say to what extent guidebooks are responsible for this. Writers like to exaggerate the impact of their pieces, and I think word of mouth is just as influential. Nevertheless, I've seen tiny fishing villages turn into big resorts and I think guide books should try to encourage sustainability over exploitation.

Can't backpackers have a positive impact on the places they visit?
Generally, backpackers stay longer in a destination, and more of their money goes to the grassroots than holidaymakers on package trips. Having said that, with cheap air travel, many just dip in and out of a place, don't really engage with it and can be just as irresponsible as many package tourists.

What qualities make a good *Rough Guide* writer?
A prodigious appetite for new places and information – you should be a bit like a sponge, absorbing all sorts of cultural and sociological information – and you must also love language, the nuts and bolts of writing. Mainly, though, you just have to cope with being on your own, and be able to put up with being broke.

Is the pay that bad?
Yes. You get paid a portion of your royalties in advance, which just about covers your expenses on the trip but not much more. After that, it just depends on how many people buy the book.

Finally, what is the question that you invariably get asked at parties, and what is your response?
'Can you get me a copy of the *Rough Guide to ... ?'* wherever they happen to be going next. I tell them to buy their own because we need the royalties.

BEN WOOD

The Independent 31 July 1999

TRIPPING FOR A LIVING

James Bedding, past winner of the Observer Young Travel Writer Award, claims work is not just one long holiday – honest

The symptoms are familiar to any travel writer: temporary loss of speech, eyeballs popping out of the head. Speech quickly returns, however, and the victim, usually a British holidaymaker that the travel writer has encountered in a bar or hotel invariably asks: 'Are you telling me you're actually paid to do this?'

Well, sort of, we say, mumbling something about the enormous amount of legwork we have to do checking out hotels and prices and how it isn't really a holiday because we're working and...

The interruption is never long in coming. 'Lucky so-and-so,' before calling over various travelling companions to share the incredulity: 'I reckon you've got the best job in the world.' We may be slow to admit it, and may take the job for granted, but there are times when every travel writer has thought, 'I can't believe I'm being paid to do this'.

I've had the thought after staying up all night watching Hindu dance-theatre and parading elephants at a temple in southern India; or feeling my ribcage throb to the beat of a hundred drummers at a samba competition in Rio; or chewing the fat with tobacco growers and cigar rollers in Cuba. I've had to pinch myself to make sure I'm really there, to remind myself how privileged I am.

'So,' comes the next question, 'how did you get into this game?' (Some spell out the subtext: 'Can I get in on this too?') Well, I was lucky enough to win *The Observer*'s Young Travel Writer of the Year competition some years back. Like the other five finalists, I'd written about a travel experience, in my case, a trip with my parents down the Nile by felucca, and my attempts to keep the journey afloat when all the captain really wanted was to stop off at the villages of each of his four wives and get stoned.

It helped that I had a passion for travel, which had taken me to Egypt to teach English, to Istanbul and Berlin.

Finalists in the Young Writers Competition will go back packing in New Zealand

And though I grew up in Sussex, I had a Swiss mother and we regularly visited her family and the spectacular, multilingual country they lived in, which meant that I could never stay for too long in a country of little Englanders, sliced white bread and drizzle.

The Observer competition certainly helped me do that. We six finalists visited the Philippines, travelling from frenetic Manila to dozy fishing villages

---

Returning home to write up a travel piece still has something of the dread of your first homework assignment in a new form at school

---

on stilts in the deep south; and when I was lucky enough to win overall, I had visions of being sent to all the exotic places I'd ever dreamed of visiting.

It took a few months of plodding on at my job in London, writing for an African magazine, travelling · extensively on the London Underground, to realise it doesn't work like that. Travel editors don't generally phone you at home and bark, 'Quick, pack your bags, you're

booked on the next flight to Honolulu!' You have to come up with fresh ideas to sell to them.

Which explains why travel writers get into some of the scrapes they do. What seems like a fun idea when you're sitting in the pub can seem well short of brilliant when you're far from home and your local casualty unit. I felt this particularly when I stood at the top of an ice chute while on a beginners' ski-jumping course in Austria, and as I shivered in a wet suit, cutting a hole in a frozen Alpine lake while learning the basics of ice diving. Or closer to home, trying to navigate a narrowboat up the Grand Union Canal, when I fell into the slimy water and found myself being squeezed between the narrowboat and the canal walls. Why hadn't I become an accountant instead? Over the years I may have had a lot more practice at being a travel writer, but the anxieties of the job somehow never fully disappear. Returning home to write up a travel piece still has something of the dread of your first homework assignment in a new form at school: Write an essay entitled, 'What I did in my holidays'. And to have a string of deadlines, one after the other, is like being reincarnated as a student with an essay crisis that never goes away. Anyone who has been a student will remember the extraordinary amount of unrelated work you get done when a deadline is looming. I feel particularly sorry for my house plants, who must now dread my deadline crises, as they surely know it means they're in for a repotting.

Sooner or later, though, there's always another trip to look forward to. And when you've got a commission to explore the distilleries of the misty Hebridean island of Islay, to taste its single malts, or to seek out the best Swiss chocolate, or to meet the Pope's ice cream maker over a bowl of the Pontiff's favourite flavour (marrons glacés) in the heart of medieval Rome, well, who's complaining? 'Jammy bastard,' they say at this point. Time to buy them a round of drinks; it's the least you can do.

The Observer 10 January 1999

Meeting *the locals*

How easy is it to be a travel writer? *John Kellie* of Kilmarnock is the winner of the Bradt travel writing competition, and was chosen by Tourism Concern as the entry showing the most insight into local issues.

Wesley Nike 2000

"Sir, what is your country?"

I groaned. In Connaught Circus this is the prelude to all kinds of hassle. I'd already had my shoes shined and my fortune told. I'd then had sacred cow dung flipped expertly over my feet and paid up for a second shoe shine. I'd declined arts, crafts, services, substances and dubious pleasures. I'd handed out small coins to legions of ragged children. The last fortnight – my first experience of the heat and paradoxes of India – had left me elated, disorientated, inspired and drained. What now?

"Welcome to India, sir. What is your country?"

He wasn't the average tout: an old man, slightly hunched, wrapped in grubby clothing; skinny frame supported by a crutch under the right arm; lifeless grey hair uncut; unkempt beard struggling up his face to peter out at prominent cheek bones. The old man was smiling. Uncertain how things might proceed. I replied "Scotland."

"Ah, dear sir! Northern Great Britain! A very beautiful country. And do you like India, sir?" The old man stepped forward.

How was I to answer? Pungent flavours; noxious odours; child beggars; pavement sleepers; Moghul treasures. I replied that India was interesting, her people friendly and the Taj Mahal beautiful. The old man seemed pleased.

"Ah, yes, sir, but we are very poor people. My family, sir, is one of the last Christian families in Rajasthan but we are very poor. Are you yourself a Christian, sir?"

I hadn't been in church since Sunday school. "Yes," I replied.

"Sir, my sons are at a very expensive Christian school. It is a great struggle, sir. We are one of the last Christian families in Rajasthan. What is your occupation in Great Britain, sir?"

I replied that I was a teacher. The old man's face lit up.

"Sir, it is a noble and honourable calling. I wish my sons to be teachers, sir. Yes, it is a noble calling, but keeping my sons in Christian school in Rajasthan is a great struggle, sir. Will you kindly give a donation, sir, to assist my sons?"

I mumbled about having an appointment, about flying home, about being a bit short of rupees.

The old man smiled sadly in the heat and darkness, his look unwavering: "Ahh, sir, I understand. You are meeting friends and leaving India tomorrow. Sir I understand." Stung, I groped in my wallet and drew out a handful of rupees. The old man received the notes graciously. "Thank you, dear sir. You assist my sons at Christian school in Rajasthan. Dear sir, thank you."

The old man made a brief dignified bow and the crowds of Connaught Circus closed over him like a curtain. ∎

Tourism Concern Winter 1999/2000

upsets

Stabbed in the back

Backpacking duo find making an insurance claim an uphill struggle

In July 1998 Tony Downing and his girlfriend, Sue, began a backpacking trip around South America, having taken out travel cover with Options Insurance Services Ltd.

Just a day after their arrival, misfortune struck, as the couple dashed for a bus outside Bogota.

As Tony climbed on the bus, he heard Sue shouting out. When he turned around to see what was going on, he felt a sharp pain in his back. He had been stabbed. His two assailants then tried to make Tony let go of his backpack by stabbing him in the wrist.

Tony heard Sue scream again, and, thinking she had been stabbed as well, he let go of the backpack. In fact, Sue had been leapt upon by the attackers, sustaining a bump to the head and several bruises.

By this time Tony felt blood oozing from his back. The bus driver rushed him to the police, who took him to hospital, where he was immediately given stitches in his back and wrist.

After Tony had given a statement to the police, he sent Options a fax explaining events and asking for advice. The ordeal had left the couple in shock, and they felt too traumatised to continue their journey by coach. In any event, Tony's back was too sore to bear a backpack.

Options told Tony and Sue that they could either be flown back to England or continue the rest of the journey by air and rail. They chose to do the latter.

When they returned to England, they made a claim on their insurance for the items that had been stolen, the mugging benefit set out in the policy, and for the additional transport costs.

Options refused to pay the mugging benefit, arguing that as the couple had been outpatients it was not due. Furthermore, it refused to pay the additional costs, alleging that it had committed itself only to considering the claim on sight of hospital reports. Tony and Sue said that they had not been told they had to obtain these, so had not done so. The insurer claimed that it had a transcript of the conversation requesting this information. Tony asked for the transcript on several occasions, to no avail.

When Options still refused to pay out, Tony and Sue asked Which? Legal Service for help.

We wrote to Options and argued that if it could

not produce the transcript supporting its case, it should either honour the claim or issue a letter of 'deadlock', so that the matter could be referred to the Insurance Ombudsman.

On receipt of our letter and in light of the harrowing and distressing circumstances, Options agreed to meet the claim.

Point of Law

If an insurance company refuses to pay out, you can sue for breach of contract. You may prefer (if the insurer belongs to the scheme) to use the free service of the Insurance Ombudsman Bureau. Its decision is binding on the insurer, but not on the policyholder.

Holiday Which? Winter 2000

Home for the holidays

The Greenwoods cut through a thicket of small print to win fair compensation

In March 1997 Margot and Jim Greenwood booked a six-week holiday at the four-star Dom Joao Hotel in the Algarve. The Airtours holiday cost £1,523, with departure on 4 January 1998.

Nine months later, on 22 December 1997, just 14 days before they were due to depart, the couple were informed by Airtours that the Dom Joao was being renovated. They were told that there would be considerable noise, including heavy drilling from 9am until 1pm and from 4pm until 6pm daily. Airtours said they could either proceed with the holiday or have their money refunded. No suitable alternative was offered. Margot and Jim had wanted a relaxing break and felt they had no option but to ask for a refund. They fully expected that they would be able to find another, similar holiday.

Despite the best efforts of their travel agent, it proved impossible to find an alternative, as all flights out of Glasgow were fully booked. Jim and

Margot had to spend their holiday at home and endure the worst excesses of the January weather.

They contacted Which? Legal Service, and we advised them to write to Airtours and claim compensation for loss of enjoyment, inconvenience, and disappointment. We pointed out that the Fair Trading Agreement in the company's booking conditions limited compensation for changes to the holiday to £40 each, but that this was open to challenge.

Airtours replied, offering them a 10 per cent discount on a future holiday, which they rejected.

We wrote to Airtours, saying that, as it would have had advance notice of the renovations, the Greenwoods were entitled to compensation for disappointment. We also pointed out that had our members cancelled their holiday within 21 days of departure, according to Airtours' Fair Trading Agreement, the operator could have retained a sum equivalent to the whole cost of the holiday – even if it was able to sell that holiday to someone else! We therefore felt it was only fair for our members to be compensated when Airtours was unable to provide the holiday booked or a suitable alternative.

Airtours finally offered £350 as a gesture of goodwill, which Margot and Jim accepted. ❷

Point of Law

Many tour operators' booking conditions contain a term that restricts your entitlement to compensation for changes. Such clauses may be unenforceable.

Holiday Which? Summer 1999

Which? and Holiday Which? published by the Consumers' Association, 2 Marylebone Road, London NW1 4DF
For further information Tel: 0800 252 100

Beaten and battered by your holiday from hell? Here's how to get compensation. By Teresa Hunter

Wish we weren't here

Hardly a dream cruise - but not all holiday troubles are as dramatic as this Channel collision

Martyn Hayhow/AFP

Dear all, having a lovely time. Smashing hotel, or it will be when it is finished. Beautiful beach, delightful trek. Disco handy, just next door. Wildlife... fascinating. Postmark Hell.

Hope triumphs over experience each year when the British set off on 16 million package holidays, only to return stressed-out and exploding with horror stories.

Disaster can strike out of the blue as it did this week when the container, Ever Decent, crashed into luxury liner, Norwegian Dream. Then again, shoddy accommodation, poor sanitation and broken promises send us scurrying for compensation.

However, this season's short-changed travellers could become caught up in the ugly storm brewing between travel firms and holiday watchdogs over how compensation should be calculated.

For months, the Association of British Travel Agents (ABTA) has been drawing up guidelines to be published shortly, aimed at helping customers prepare claims. This week, however, in a dramatic counter-attack, trading standards chiefs dismissed the travel industry's offensive as 'irrelevant' and warned holidaymakers they were unlikely to be a true reflection of their legal rights.

An ABTA spokesman explains: 'Some people think they can have a full refund when just one element proves unsatisfactory. They can't.'

Holiday firms think some customers have unrealistic expectations about what they can claim in damages when something goes wrong. The new guidelines aim to curtail those expectations, thereby limiting the damages bill.

An ABTA spokesman explains: 'Some people think they can have a full refund when just one element proves unsatisfactory. They can't.'

He says flights typically account for 60 per cent of most package deals, so even if your accommodation is appalling, you are unlikely to receive as much as 40 per cent back. Similarly, the cost of providing a swimming pool would be a tiny fraction of the bill. The loss of that pool would be equally insignificant when calculating a payment.

But the Institute of Trading Standards, which polices the industry, strongly disagrees. Its chief officer Ed Chicken says: 'It is wholly irrelevant to the holidaymaker how much the tour operator pays for

Travel Matters © Carel Press

flights. Compensation should be based on the impact on the customers' enjoyment of their whole package if something falls short. It may be miserable to be stuck in an airport for 12 hours because of a flight delay, but if that is followed by 12 or 13 days of blissful holiday, people quickly forget. It is much more miserable to be stuck for two weeks in a cockroach- infested villa.'

There are no laws on the amount of compensation, although ABTA says its guidelines will follow normal court procedure. Its spokesman said: 'The courts look at the various components of a holiday and make an award based on the value of that part of the package.'

Not so, says Ed Chicken, adding: 'The courts look at what you've received for what you have spent. If something goes wrong so that one day of your holiday is ruined, then you can reasonably claim the value of that day. But if something like poor accommodation ruins your entire holiday, then you are not only entitled to the full cost back, but additional compensation for the loss of your one opportunity of a good holiday until next year.'

So how do you complain about your holiday from hell? Your contract is with the tour operator so first approach the company at the resort via the rep. If the promises in the brochure were misleading, or some aspect of the trip is ruined through negligence or maladministration, you have a legitimate claim. However, you also have a legal duty to mitigate damages by giving the firm a chance to put things right on the spot. If you are still dissatisfied on your return, you should write immediately to the travel company, which must reply within 28 days. If you still get no joy, then you must write again, before you can approach ABTA's arbitration service.

For a flat fee of £65, ABTA will assess your claim, and 80 per cent of those who go to arbitration win. Worryingly, however, only 1,625 of the initial 18,400 complaints made last year went to arbitration. Alternatively, you could consider legal action through the County Court small claims procedure, for disputes under £3,000.

Do not be bullied by the company. The timetable for publishing these tough new guidelines has been slipping all summer, and if Trading Standards get their way, they may never see the light of day.

An ABTA spokesman reluctantly admits it is a very delicate exercise, which would have to be sensitively worded.

'In fact, you could say we're only really at the planning stage,' he adds.

For further information contact: Association of British Travel Agents, 55-57 Newman Street, London. Tel: 020 7637 2444).

The Independent 28 August 1999

HOW TO MAKE THEM PAY

- Last minute changes to hotel, itinerary or destination are breach of contract. Demand full refund or an alternative holiday.

- Always complain first to the tour rep. If it is not sorted out quickly, ask for a company complaint form.

- Take photos or videos of poor accommodation or building work.

- If you incur extra expenses because of breach of contract, get receipts or bills as proof.

- Keep a record of problems with dates and action taken.

- Ask other travellers if they will back up your complaint.

- Back home, write to the tour operator's head office and say what compensation you want.

- Enclose copies of documentary evidence, photos, receipts, bills.

- Keep the originals in case you need them for any future action.

- Be persistent! Don't allow yourself to be fobbed off with excuses. If you are not happy with the initial reply, you should complain to your local Trading Standards department.

'Total physical and mental inertia are highly agreeable, much more so than we allow ourselves to imagine. A beach not only permits such inertia but enforces it, thus neatly eliminating all problems of guilt. It is now the only place in our overly active world that does.'
J K Galbraith

TED, 10, IS A TINY TERROR

ARMY-mad youngster Ted Hills was arrested by cops in Barbados because they said his camouflage clothes made him look like a **TERRORIST**.

The ten-year-old lad was stunned when security men marched him off to be interrogated minutes after stepping off the plane in his favourite Marks & Spencer's T-shirt, trousers and fleece top.

Then two stern-faced officials ordered him to take off the clothes saying it was an offence in Barbados to wear fatigues. Astonished mum Pat, 48, of Stockport, Greater Manchester, said: "I told them he was no terrorist but they didn't listen.

"They told him to change into normal T-shirt and shorts before letting us through."

Ted, who wants to join the SAS, said: "It was amazing — I'd never been mistaken for a terrorist."

The Sun 28 January 1999

Photo: Stockport Express

Travel Matters © Carel Press

Pardon my French, but c'est une liberté

Andrew Anthony languished in a French language school in Languedoc, stuck on his imperfect subjunctives. But not until he had a bust-up with his landlord did he truly find his foreign tongue

When a British person is asked by the French if he or she speaks their language the polite answer is always: 'Un petit peu.' For a few lucky souls this translates as being able to discuss the poetry of Rimbaud with effortless fluency while, in a faultless accent, ordering a bottle of Chateauneuf-du-Pape, Cuvée de Sommeliers dix-neuf cent vingt-quatre dix – Mestre. For the majority of us, though, it's more likely to mean the ability to say the phrase 'un petit peu'.

Unfortunately, the French often take our good-mannered response as a green-light to indulge their unintelligible tongue, at which point, naturally, we become frozen in uncomprehending silence. Having been thrown out of O-level French in the fourth year, this linguistic paralysis has long dogged my forays across the Channel. Last October, I decided that at the age of 36 it was time to do something about it.

Owed a month's sabbatical, I resolved to immerse myself in a four-week language course in France. I researched the choices on offer, which is to say, I looked at the courses available in the South of France, where it would still be sunny and warm in autumn and where I could sit drinking coffee and eating fresh croissants in pleasant squares. I thought the Côte D'Azur would be too expensive and a friend mentioned Montpellier. I phoned up the local Alliance Française and booked a place.

That was that. I sent a deposit of 700 francs (about £77), and the Alliance reserved a 'studio' flat for me. The braver option would have been to live with a family for a month. But that seemed to my mind needlessly, indeed recklessly, keen. The thought of being interrogated on a nightly basis by sturdy members of the provincial bourgeoisie, and in French, was simply too much to contemplate. Happily, Madame Leroux, who runs the Alliance in Montpellier, agreed.

Two weeks later, courtesy of a nifty Eurostar and TGV combination, I arrived in Languedoc's largest city, which lies about seven miles from the Mediterranean coast, in France's south-west corner. My studio was in the old city, the semi-walled centre of Montpellier. As I negotiated my way through its narrow streets on a mild evening, I was struck by how different it was to the chocolate box France of Aix-en-Provence or Arles.

Not since the 'Bash-the-Rich' marches of the eighties had I seen so many crusties gathering in one place, with their obligatory dog on a string. I can't pretend that I was overjoyed to see young men with lots of facial hair urinating in the street, but I thought it at least made a change from French teenagers on mopeds pretending to be Americans. The novelty soon wore off, however, after the third time I was beerily asked for some change.

The landlord met me outside my studio above a Pizza restaurant, and showed me round a room with bare concrete walls, a two-ring stove and a single mattress that was the opposite of orthopaedic. He spoke in rapid French backed up by elaborate gestures. I nodded a lot. For 2,500 francs (plus 500 francs deposit) I wasn't complaining. All the same, that evening I sat looking at a French text book and thought: 'What have I done?'

The next morning I took an hour-long test at the Alliance to determine the level of French I would study. I say an hour, but I had run out of things to write after about 20 minutes, and had to watch

as intense teenagers with colour-coded felt-tips teased out the more subtle uses of the imperfect subjunctive tense. I assumed that they would have to invent a new category for me: pre-beginner. But Mme Leroux, an elegantly formidable matriarch, advised me that I should take the beginner's grammar class and the intermediate's oral. As I suspected, this was a slightly generous interpretation of my language skills. Not least because in the intermediate class the students could speak French, or at least something that sounded like it, whereas I was still at the 'petit peu' stage.

The classes ran for three hours from 9am with a 15-minute break. This arrangement seemed ideal as it allowed for plenty of coffee drinking in the sun.

There was also time to explore the town. Montpellier is run by one of those far-sighted local authorities that put their British equivalents to shame. As well as managing to maintain their historic centre in a manner that makes it a vibrant part of the city rather than some heritage museum, the municipal government has built an ambitious housing estate in the Antigone district that would be the envy of any council. It has elegant apartments, excellent shops and the best swimming pool I have ever seen.

My grammar class taught by a wonderful teacher named Delphine, was a treat but I was struggling in the oral. It wasn't, however, until I relegated myself to the beginner's oral class that I learned that it was possible to possess yet more basic French than mine. The optimum class size is probably about eight to 10, but we had nearer 15, and one kid from the Oman who obviously didn't want to be studying at all.

After a few days of repeating phrases like 'C'est combien, s'il vous plaît?', I realised that I would have to find a one-

> The landlord spoke in rapid French backed up by elaborate gestures. I nodded a lot.

on-one lesson if I was to progress at the rate I had hoped. Mme Leroux poo-pooed the idea, and said that all I needed to do was meet some French people in a bar and, in a manner of speaking, get stuck in.

There were two problems with this theory. One, of course, was the French: they are not in the habit of talking to strangers in bars, particularly those whose conversational gambits are restricted to asking them how old they are and where they live. The other was me: I needed a captive, preferably paid, audience, to feel confident enough to express my limited vocabulary.

Montpellier is a university town full of private tutors and it wasn't difficult to find one for £15 an hour. I dropped out of the morning oral class and took an afternoon lesson with an enthusiastic woman on the rue de Universitie. It was unstructured and probably not ideal but at least I'd found a guaranteed space in which to speak French.

In the morning, I listened to the radio in my concrete shell. At lunch I pretended to read a newspaper in one of the many little squares in the old town where you could find a three-course meal for about £6. The one drawback to this remarkable bargain was the buskers. Montpellier has the worst street entertainers in the world: drunk, tuneless and persistent. It was a daily pleasure not to give them money. In the evening I went to the cinema – there was a choice of three multi-screens in the main square alone.

Mme Leroux had encouraged this mediated approach, and I liked the idea of almost passively absorbing a language. In practice, I clung to the occasional passing phrase that I could catch like a non-swimmer grabs hold of floating debris.

The dry land of comprehension was still a long way off. After two weeks, I knew that I was not going to be the fluent sophisticate of my dreams. I suspected I was one of those people genetically incapable of learning a language. But if so, I was in a class full of them. Indeed I was the best student. The other explanation was that, unless you are unfairly gifted, it takes time to enter a new language and find your way around. And the older you are, the longer it takes.

To compensate for this dispiriting realisation, I hired a car and took off for a weekend. Sete is France's largest fishing port on the Med, but it's also charmingly unpretentious and surprisingly attractive. Along the banks of a canal, which runs through the centre of town, are some of the finest, and cheapest, seafood restaurants, you'll find anywhere in France.

Also within easy reach was the Disney-like walled-city of Carcassone. It looks like a medieval fantasy-land and, in a sense, it is. Although they date back as far as the Romans, the ramparts and towers were 'restored' by the 19th century architect Viollet-le-Duc. Even so, it's still a magical site. Another weekend included a visit to the Carmargue, the eerie marshlands of the Rhone delta famed for their wild horses, and Arles, which has a wonderful melancholy beauty in autumn, very different from its packed and sweaty summer self.

Back at school in my last week, I was filled with mixed emotions. I was pleased that I'd made the snap decision to study French but a little annoyed with myself that I hadn't taken a bit more time researching my choice. For the price,

just under £300, the Alliance was perfectly reasonable. However, I felt that I would have been prepared to spend a little more money for classes with fewer students. I was also beginning to think that perhaps a preparatory course in England would have been handy. If I'd arrived with some form of working grammar, I could have got to the more interesting stage of conversation – that is, actually having one – much more quickly. But. But. But. It was a start. And I could always take a follow-up class back home, I reasoned.

In the end, the month had gone rapidly and I was a little reluctant to leave. I hadn't achieved what I had wanted but I was beginning to see the way ahead. The measure of my improvement was the chat I had with the landlord when it came to reclaiming my 500 franc deposit.

He visited me the night before I left and immediately went into a dramatic fit about the state of the studio. It was immaculate, of course, but he pointed to some ancient stains on the carpet. I couldn't believe he was trying to pull such a low-down trick and momentarily I was stunned into silence.

Then suddenly, it happened, I was shouting at him in French, finding words that I didn't even know that I knew to vocalise my disgust. 'Pardon monsieur,' I explained, 'mais je croix que vous devez beaucoup vouloir mon argent. Parce que vous savez que ces taches sont tres vieux. C'est insupportable!' And so on.

It wasn't, of course, grammatically correct, but it worked. 'Ah,' he said, brightening, 'vous parlez Francais.' And he handed me the 500 franc note.

The Observer
17 January 1999

> I clung to the occasional passing phrase that I could catch like a non-swimmer grabs hold of floating debris.

> Then suddenly it happened. I was shouting at him in French.

P eter M cKay

Going for a Chinese

When my parents came to visit me in Chengdu, the capital of Sichuan province, I did as the Sichuanese do and invited them out for a meal of the fiery local hotpot. My Chinese friends and I guzzled tripe, kidneys and other offal with cheerful abandon. It was only when I noticed my father struggling politely with a rubbery goose intestine that I realised how much my own tastes had been changed by China.

Somewhere along the way in my encounter with China, I made the decision to eat absolutely anything. It was probably when some delightful new acquaintance placed in my rice bowl an unfamiliar bit of bird or beast, and I was faced with the stark choice of acting like a foreigner, or challenging my own ideas of what was edible.

Accepting food and drink is a way of showing respect for people wherever you go. But in China it's especially important. No other culture has such a long, such a rich, such an astonishing tradition of gastronomy. Chinese poets and philosophers have mused for centuries, millennia even, on the pleasures of eating; Chinese emperors had legions of staff attending to their diet; and they even say one imperial cook won such royal favour that he became prime minister.

Psychologists have also found that a traditional fear of heated emotions means Chinese people tend to express love and affection in indirect, physical ways. When I wept once in a Chinese class my teacher didn't ask me what was wrong – she just gave me candied fruits and walnuts to feed my brain. And Chinese friends never kiss me goodbye – they're more likely to send me on my way with some special tea leaves or a bag of apples.

Mainland Chinese people often expect Westerners to be totally alien and incapable of relating to them on a personal level. China, after all, only reopened to the outside world twenty years ago, and many Chinese people still haven't had the chance to talk to a foreigner. Often they assume that, coming as I do from a developed country, I will look down on China and its culture as impoverished and backward. Sharing food was my way of telling people that this wasn't so, and that I was willing to meet them without making too much of the inevitable cultural differences.

Of course if one is going to eat everything, China is one of the most difficult places in the world to do it. There's a saying about the Cantonese which goes: Of all that flies in the sky, the only thing they don't eat is the

aeroplane; of all that runs on the ground the only thing they don't eat is the ship. It's not a great exaggeration, and in my time in China, that's pretty much what I've done too. I've eaten scorpions and snakes, dog's meat and chicken's feet, drunk the gall of a snake in a glass of rice wine.

Sometimes my resolve has been tested, like the time I was invited into a restaurant kitchen to watch the preparation of a spicy rabbit dish. When I entered, the main ingredient, sweet and fluffy, was nibbling lettuce at the side of the room. I had to watch while it was stunned, skinned alive and then chopped into tiny pieces. Less than ten minutes later it was sitting in a bowl of sauce on the table in front of me. I didn't feel like eating, but when I looked at the smile of expectant pleasure on the face of my friend, who had so kindly invited me to lunch, I set aside all thought of protest, raised my chopsticks, and ate.

Of course compromising one's own cultural identity has its price. You can't expose yourself to another culture without losing something of your own identity. Long acquaintance with the squawking, wriggling markets of central China has definitely changed my view of food, as I realised once on a solitary walk in the English countryside. I passed a field of geese, which a few years ago I would have enjoyed as part of the rural scene. This time, before I knew it, I was imagining them braised in a sauce of salted beans and chillies, bubbling away on a gas burner.

I've lost my European distaste for slithery and crunchy textures, which I now enjoy, and I have to make myself remember what my English friends won't eat when we dine together in Chinese restaurants. And I can no longer bring myself to buy fish in my local London market – I haven't killed them myself or seen them slaughtered, so I know they won't be what a Chinese person would consider fresh.

But breaking all the boundaries of European taste has also been a revelation. I'm constantly astounded by the resourcefulness of Chinese cooking, its ability to transform clumsy offal into marvellous delicacies; its use of obscure fungi and wild leafy plants, its medicinal secrets and seasonal variations. And adding texture to the sensory delights of colour, smell and taste has made eating even more exciting than it was before.

By comparison, European cooking seems strangely limited and wasteful.

We tend unconsciously to insulate ourselves against a real encounter with another culture. Aren't all those water-purifying pills and vaccinations a little more than just technical, a way of reminding ourselves we're venturing into the dangerous unknown? Of course, it's easier to keep up the cultural barriers, like those backpackers who breakfast on toast and honey from Boston to Beijing. But before you can really experience the joy of knowing something completely different, perhaps you have to give up a little of yourself.

August Fuchsia Dunlop
From Our Own Correspondent
13 August 1999
BBC Radio 4

Letter from Mongolia

A Frozen World

Louisa Waugh experiences Mongolia's winter

I WAKE UP AND MY WORLD HAS FROZEN. Everything, and I mean everything, my water, tomato paste, soap – is encased in thick, milky ice. I light a candle, stand up in my sleeping bag and pull on another layer of clothing. Shivering, I take a knife to the water bucket and hack at the ice until bubbles rise to the surface. Lighting my small stove is tough because the wood, which was damp, is now frozen.

By the time my smoky fire is finally crackling and heating the water and ice in the kettle, the outside temperature has risen to -25 degrees centigrade. I've never been so cold in my life. I know the

mountains surrounding my village will be drenched in fresh snow and the sun rising late, but I can't see anything because my window is coated in thick ice.

On the dark, freezing winter morning, venturing to the communal outside toilet is quite an endurance test. But, after two cups of steaming black coffee I am bundled up and off to work, just as the sky is gradually brightening.

My school is a ten-minute walk alongside the Hovd river which flows through the village. The river is now so solid that horses are being ridden and cars driven over it. Everything but my eyes is concealed from the freezing air – my gloved fingers pushed down into my pockets.

'Louisa – off to work?' calls my neighbour Sansar-Huu. 'Don't worry,' he teases me, 'it's quite warm today – just wait till it gets really cold!'

Our school has no electricity or running water, but each small classroom is heated by a wood-burning stove. This morning we all wear our coats during lessons. Wind-burnt children from herders' settlements outside the village board at the school, 12 to a dormitory. Their parents pay the fees in meat and wood.

At break, we jostle to be near the staff-room stove and my colleagues pull their fur hats back on. 'You sit by the fire, Louisa – you must be freezing,' offers Sansar-Huu's wife Gansukh, my fellow English teacher. I am.

After our classes Gansukh and I cross the street to the post office, which is crowded as the weekly post has just arrived. Beaming and clutching two letters I walk home with Gansukh and a couple of our students, passing herders

trading camel, sheep, goat and wolf skins. We stop en route for bowls of tea at a friend's house. At home, I need more water. Armed with a bucket, I lift the creaking lid of the well opposite our yard. But the water is so frozen I can hear the rocks I fling down the shaft ricochet off the ice. Taking the axe I set out for the nearby river to forge my own well.

That afternoon it snows heavily as Sansar-Huu and I saw logs in the yard. 'How long will it be this cold?' I ask him as I stand panting, my face flushed and numb. 'Oh, it gets as low as -48° here,' he tells me, grinning. 'But we need this snowy winter. Even in October it's really too cold to live in a felt *ger* here – so the herders in the mountains move up into their winter log cabins. Their livestock live on hay and the herders melt snow for all their water. They slaughter sheep and cows for food at the start of winter, when the animals are still fat and the ice stores the meat till the end of spring.'

'So, if the snow comes late, like it did this year, what then?' I query, resting on a white log. 'That's when the steppe gets overgrazed, which means spring will be very tough. Remember those trucks loaded up with ice driving way into the mountains?' I nod. 'The ice was for herders who didn't have enough snow and weren't near the rivers.'

Sansar-Huu pauses to wave and call greetings to a local who trots past, his horse crusted in frozen sweat. I look around me at the snowscape – silent mountains on all four sides, pack camels weighed down with flour and hay, children skating on the river – and the deep, untrodden snow.

I pick up the axe and raise it to my shoulder just as Sansar-Huu turns back to me.

'You know,' he says, 'the herders are fine now – the snow is here for the winter. Oh, we'll be waiting for spring and warmer weather to arrive – but hopefully not too soon.'

Louisa Waugh *lives and works in Mongolia and is writing a book about Mongolian life.*

New Internationalist March 1999

> The outside temperature has risen to -25 degrees centigrade. I've never been so cold in my life.

e-mail from Tokyo

Home truths. By Mrs Moneypenny

FLYING FOR 22 hours from London to Sydney was not enough. A week after his arrival, citing his better-than-usual school report, my 10-year-old begged me to let him visit his friend in Adelaide as a reward. I groaned, not just because of the expense, but because I knew that when I rang the airline, I would have to give them my credit card billing address in Japan.

Explaining a Japanese address to someone not based in Japan is always stressful. Addresses in Japan are full of hyphens and numbers, as well as unfamiliar-sounding districts. They also do not enable you to find the house or flat they describe.

Japanese addresses identify the district in which

one lives by name, but this merely narrows the area down to several square kilometres. The three digits attached to the name give greater clues. The first of these identifies the 'chome' or subdistrict, and is usually the extent of any taxi driver's knowledge, being a mere two square kilometres or so.

The second digit tells you which part of the subdistrict the property is in, which means you are down to about half a square kilometre. The final part is the hardest – the third digit. This refers to the plot of land on which the property is built, and these are numbered in the order in which they were built. Therefore, plot 25 will be nowhere near plot 24, and may have several houses located on it. Our address is shared by no less than five other houses.

Of course, this anachronism of Japanese life means that telephoning for a pizza or inviting

> **Explaining a Japanese address to someone not based in Japan is always stressful**

people round for dinner becomes an entirely new challenge. In Tokyo, more so than anywhere in the world, people rely on both the fax machine and the work of thousands of amateur cartographers. If you order a pizza from a place you haven't used before, you will have to fax them a map of how to find you.

Maps are to be found on the back of business cards, and in advertisements for shops – in fact, everywhere, usually in both Japanese and English. It is unusual to find an expatriate who doesn't have a home 'meishi' (business card), complete with a map on the back of how to find them. No wonder the Japanese install global positioning systems in their cars as a matter of course.

Tourists, bloody tourists

You're messy, you're badly dressed and you don't spend enough. You know who you are.

By John Walsh and Frances Kennedy

Venice's campaign, in association with Colors magazine and Benetton, highlights the effect of the 12 million tourists who visit every year. The photo shows Venice the day after the Pink Floyd Concert. Photo: Arici/Grazianeri

Bloody tourists. Here they come, droves and droves of them, flooding into town on buses and trains and package-deal coaches, multitudes of stumbling, shuffling, clicking, chattering, philistine, half-witted, snack-munching, funny-hat-wearing, peeling-nosed, uniglottal, rucksack-toting strangers with designs on your town, your proud city, your beloved backyard.

But the designs they have are limited. They do not want to spend days getting to know you. They will not spend hours drinking in the view over the harbour, or gazing respectfully at the Tintorettos on the ceiling. They will almost certainly not spend £100 on a decent meal with bottles of the local red wine. They're supposed to be bolstering the fortunes of local business, but they're showing increasing reluctance to do so. They're becoming a liability, a drain on local resources, a threat to the environment, a nuisance.

Stories of brawling in dance-halls, broken beer bottles on the beach, topless tits in Côte d'Azur gift shops, litter in the street and puke in the pool have abounded this summer, as such stories abound every summer. They've been joined by a comparatively recent upsurge in fake insurance claims by British people (like the man from Bournemouth who claimed that thousands of pounds worth of scuba-diving equipment had been nicked from a Marbella hotel; the Costa police looked suspiciously at his beer gut, discovered he had no diving licence and found that he's made 25 similar claims in six years).

Tourism rules. Everyone knows that. You can't argue with the figures. The inhabitants of St Lucia or Rio or Shanghai or Bath may suffer momentary feelings of invasion by yet more hordes in acid-green cagouls, but they will put up with it for a greater good: visitors' money...

Until now, that is. A cloud of unrest has been gathering. Murmurs of discontent that go back years have begun to crescendo, and they are saying one thing: Tourists Go Home.

A few weeks ago, St Tropez, the top fleshpot of the French Riviera, decided it had had enough. In high summer the flood of visitors can reach 100,000 a day in this small town with a population of 5,600. Now the mayor, Jean-Michel Couve, has set up a commission to work with environmental groups and tour operators to improve the quality of life for residents who are upset by the noise, the litter and psychic debris of the summer invasion. 'The St Tropez of the Fifties is finished,' said one of the commission members. 'Every day dozens of coaches disgorge hundreds of daytrippers who wander round the village buying cans of soft drinks and fast food, which they drop in the street.'

St Trop is not alone. In Deauville and Cannes, shopkeepers have barred holidaymakers if they're dressed only in bathing costume and flip-flops. In Trouville, topless pedestrians of both sexes are banned. In Brittany, you're now not allowed to consume alcohol on the beach. (There are rumours that mobile phones will be next.)

Across Europe, a cloud of exasperation has begun to rain on the visitors' parade. On the Costa del Sol, Spanish police are clamping down on tourists' reports of lost property and muggings; mendacious claimants will now face jail. In Cyprus, the police go one better: any tourist who reports the theft of his property is likely to wind up being interrogated for six hours. In Florence, they've begun to clamp down on the number of coaches allowed into the centre, and the Uffizi Gallery (like the Alhambra in Spain) has been forced to restrict access to popular artworks – a startling precedent.

In Venice, a whole tourist counter-revolution appears to be brewing. Consider, for instance, the poster that greets visitors to the main vaporetto stop near Santa Lucia station. It shows a rubber sink plunger, its handle in the form of the white-and-red-striped mooring poles that symbolise Venice, and it carries the legend, 'Thank you for shopping in Venice'. It's part of a campaign commissioned by the city's mayor, Massimo Cacciari, and carried out by Fabrica, the art workshop sponsored by Benetton, and directed by Oliviero Toscani. The campaign is entitled 'For Venice Against Venice', and the photos are published in the latest edition of Colors magazine. The intention is to highlight the impact of 12 million visitors to the city every year and to focus attention on the very real problems of this unique city. Toscani, famous for his shocking ad campaigns for Benetton, describes the work as a 'starting point for talking about Venice in a different way'.

But some people believe the images – of two dogs mating in the main square, a tourist being attacked by pigeons, a roll of loo paper with the trade mark 'Venice Lion' on it, a dead rat – go too far. Even Cacciari, who had specifically asked Toscani for a campaign that was not just déjà vu clichés, drew the line at some of the stronger images.

A native Venetian, Cacciari has himself often criticised the effects of tourism, lamenting the stream of day-trippers who tramp through the streets, leaving litter and spending paltry sums in fast-food outlets or at the best cheap trattorie. Many tour operators lodge their groups on the mainland or in neighbouring cities, and come over for the day. Cacciari wants the city to be a vital living entity, not just a sort of theme park, a cluster of churches, palaces, museums and cafes to be 'done' by tourists who then move on.

The campaign has divided local politicians and residents – of whom one in seven depends on tourism for a living. The tourism manager (appointed by the mayor) was reported to be vehemently opposed.

'I think the posters are disgraceful,' said the owner of a shop selling over-the-top and over-priced Murano glassware. 'When the Serb war was on and Venetian fishermen were hauling in cluster bombs, we were all terrified that this summer no one would come. Now we are trying to turn them away.'

A woman serving at a tiny lace-curtained wine bar commented: 'I am in favour. We have to put up with the problems all year round – they just come, drink their mineral water on the church steps, and then get back on the bus.'

Perhaps the most radical initiative in this legendary day-trippers' destination is the anti-tourism tour. Every weekend throughout August, Greenpeace has been offering a guided tour to the 'other' Venice, the grim industrial heartland which few tourists ever see. It's called 'The Dark Side of Venice Tour'. For 10,000 lire – just over £3 – visitors can see the sights which Greenpeace says are threatening the existence of the lagoon, the city of Venice and its inhabitants.

When is Great Britain going to join in the continental drift against the summer migrants? The city that's leading the way is Cambridge (population 120,000; annual tourist invasion 3.5 million), where a recent city council report stresses the need to 'minimise the impact of tourism, particularly on the daily lives of local people'. They're fed up, it seems, with what they call the Look and Lick brigade, who descend from coaches for two hours, gawp at King's College, ingest a 99 Flake and leave without spending any money. A 10-point plan suggests that tourists are encouraged to stick around and visit surrounding districts such as Ely, Newmarket and Saffron Walden.

Is this the beginning of a British backlash? Can we envisage a ban (oh blissful vision) on the tourist coaches that routinely (and illegally) park all the way along the Thames Embankment and Park Lane? Could we anticipate a selection process whereby only certain visitors are allowed to inspect the Rembrandts at the National Gallery? Will tourists be discouraged from drinking beer on Margate Sands? Somehow, you just know it's not going to happen.

The Independent 24 August 1999

Travel sickness © Ros Asquith

The Guardian 15 January 2000

'There are some disagreeable things in Venice' *wrote Henry James*, but 'nothing so disagreeable as the visitors.'

'Too many people in the piazza, too many limbs and trunks of humanity on the Lido, too many motor launches, too many steamers, too many pigeons, too many ices, too many cocktails, too many manservants wanting tips, too many languages rattling, too much sun, too much smell of Venice, too many cargoes of strawberries, too many silk-shawls, too many huge slices of water-melon on stalls: too much enjoyment, altogether far too much enjoyment.'
D H Lawrence
Lady Chatterley's Lover (1928)

NOT RAVING BUT CLOWNING

Rory Carroll joins the Ibiza clubbers and finds the lurid media reports tell only part of the story.

Photo: Rex

Four in the morning in San Antonio's West End and the wildlife comes out to play. Beer bottles smash on to the pavement but the human swarm hears nothing over the music pounding from bars.

The doors of the Nightlife disco open and two young men barrel past the bouncers, vomit smeared on their bare chests. They embrace, then wrestle, then soil each other's hair.

Five teenage girls watch and applaud until one is grabbed by a bouncer and carried on his shoulders up the steps. One of her friends lunges to try and pull down the exposed knickers. The bouncer whirls and his captive's knee-high white boots catch the lunger in the face. She howls. At the bottom of the street four lads sing: 'No surrender to the IRA' while their friend shakes a sapling. It refuses to crack so he kicks it and urinates instead.

Round the corner the 24-hour first-aid station gets another arrival; a 17-year-old Lancastrian with a bloodied face and shirt and panic in his eyes. It is the first time he has been beaten up.

Two olive uniformed Guardia Civil policemen sit in their squad car and stare straight ahead, expressionless. A drunk is leaning in their window demanding directions to the 'cathouse'. He says he's also a policeman and entitled to a discount.

Dennis Mackessy, aged 27, looks around nervously and makes a confession. 'I've been all round the world and I've never been afraid to tell people I'm Irish. But this lot are unbelievable, I can't open my gob.' Three skinheads swagger towards Fernando Dominguez, 18, a tiny kitchen porter from Capone's Chippy. He sees them, drops his bag of rubbish and scuttles into a doorway.

The local paper has branded them animals

This was yesterday morning, just another day in what passes for routine in San Antonio, a seaside town in the northwest of Ibiza. A maelstrom was enveloping the revellers, but they were too drunk to know or care. The local paper, Diario Ibiza, had branded them animals, and pushed Michael Birkett over the edge: the United Kingdom's official representative on the island had quit in disgust at his countrymen's depravity. His resignation became official yesterday morning, unleashing a torrent of media abuse against the revellers.

They had turned a paradise into the Gomorrah of the Med and dragged Britain's reputation through the mud. Diplomacy evaporated from Birkett, 51, a vice-consul paid to look after them. They were degenerates, out of control, he fumed. Birkett's prescription, at least as reported by a Sunday tabloid, was a measure of his ire: the miscreants, he suggested, should be gassed.

Looking out at the passing hordes, the receptionist at the Piscis Park Hotel spoke so softly it was difficult to hear. 'I hate them, I really hate them. The English behave like pigs, they respect nothing, they know nothing.' The hotel's guests, like the rest of the town, were 80 per cent British.

The receptionist's eyes followed a guest leading in her catch, a good looking boy in trainers and jeans. 'You think they care that I hate them? They don't care.' He was wrong. The couple, it turned out, did care. 'There's a real community here,' Denise explained later. 'I've been coming here for five years now and these people are like my family. To make us out to be some form of ravers – I hate that word – is just so unfair. Our parents read that word and think horrible things about us but in fact we're just here to have a good time.' To understand the apparent contradiction between the receptionist's contempt and the apparent sensitivity of British visitors like Denise, you need to understand that there are two Ibizas. Turn right out of the hotel and a two minute walk takes you to the West End, a strip of a few dozen bars teeming with the over-dressed grist of the package holiday mill. But turn left out of the hotel and you reach another Ibiza, mellower and populated only by the more stylish and athletic of the island's visitors.

Here British people don't drink until they vomit, don't fight and squawk and try to pull down knickers. The fact that they appear to be the vast majority is even more surprising. Look deeper and something else emerges. Even those in the West End aren't widely despised after all. Ibiza's natives have not turned against them. Behind the puke and sweat they see a more complex picture in which the louts are ordinary kids manipulated by a voracious industry.

William Crichton, 38, knows something about it. Half Spanish and half Californian, he owns Bar M, a two minute moped ride from the West End. 'Most of those who come are clubbers. That means they don't drink too much, maybe a little Red Bull and vodka. They're aesthetes, they care how they look.

'The clubbers have revived the spirit of the artists who settled here in the fifties. That ethos died in the eighties, until club culture arrived. It's a mass movement and Ibiza has become its world centre. The energy it brings is something very positive.

'There are assholes who come here to get drunk and fall over but they do that everywhere. It depresses me that the media have always picked up on the West End and applied it to the whole island. Is all of Britain like Newcastle on a Saturday night? The English are probably the most sophisticated. They don't have the arrogance of the Germans and they don't try to get away with murder like the Italians, who will do anything to get away without paying.' An off-duty policeman agrees: 'The English are fine. There are lots of them so you will always get some trouble, but that was the way with the Scandinavians 15 years ago.' The theory of clubbers' good behaviour wobbles at the entrance to the SES Paradis nightclub. A boy is pushing a girl's T-shirt over her breasts and his tongue begins to flick. She turns around to squirm in his lap and seconds later he appears to relax. Inside the vast cavernous interior, the decor is all mock Greco-Roman and naked bodies gyrate on TV screens. Orgiastic hedonism could scarcely find better quarters, yet the

hundreds of toned bodies do nothing more than dance. Few dance with, let alone touch, each other.

Shouting above the music Danny Drew, 21, from Sussex, says no-one is drunk. 'It's too expensive, but that's not why we're here anyway. You just bring your bottle of water and refill it.' It was impossible to gauge how many of the ecstatic dancers were fuelled by the tablets on sale outside. Few males bothered to stare for long at the girl in spangly red hotpants and boob tube gyrating on the platform: they were concentrating on their own moves. Inside the gents there was no one preening in front of the mirror.

One girl nodded sadly when told of Birkett's resignation. 'That's thanks to those fat fools in the West End. Check them out and you'll see what I mean.' Which takes us back to the bare-chested young men gleaming with vomit outside the Nightlife nightclub. A gruesome spectacle, for sure, but look closer. Andreas, 38, the Spanish bouncer, is checking that they're okay. Satisfied they are only larking, he returns to the door and excuses their behaviour. 'They get sick, so what? As long as they're not violent it's okay. We need these people, without them we've no work. What then?' Further up the street Dominguez, the skinny kitchen porter, says he's cowering in the doorway not to evade skinheads but because he's spotted an ex-girlfriend.

At the first-aid station Dr Basil Safar, the head of San Antonio's accident and emergency unit, says his beaten-up Lancastrian patient is highly unusual. Traffic accidents, food poisoning and pensioners' frailty provides his regular workload. He scoffs at media reports that 50 Britons die on Ibiza each year: 'No way. One a month maybe, usually a heart attack or moped crash.' He is mellow about the drinking. 'When I was 17 I had my stomach pumped. I was stupid, we're all stupid at this age. Anyway we only do about one stomach pump a fortnight.' Safar can't understand the fuss over Birkett. 'It's just kids.' Mackessy, the nervous Irishman, has another confession. 'The English aren't as bad as they're painted. Hundreds of them watched the Liverpool-Newcastle match in the pub and there wasn't a glass raised in anger.' Even the passed-out drunks were partly exculpated by Antoni Mari Tur, the Mayor of San Antonio. 'They are kids away from home going crazy, but the ones I blame are the tour operators. They used to take commission only from the hotels, now they take it from bars and discos.' Vouchers, flyers, excursions and discounts were being used to push them into bars and keep them there with the collusion of bar owners. Clubbers at Ibiza airport complained they had been ripped off by operators' representatives. The mayor said he was mystified by

yesterday's publicity. He suggested Birkett was temperamentally unsuited to a job involving young people. 'It's better now than five years ago. Young British people are normal.' A point echoed by Cristina Amanda Tur, the Diario Ibiza reporter whose 'animals' comparison was cited in yesterday's newspapers as a sweeping condemnation. 'I only meant a tiny minority, not the ordinary English. I don't know why the press got so excited.' Among the clubbers, the curious affair of Our Man in Ibiza was debated with wry nonchalance. No-one was surprised by his outburst, they said. Ibiza had a knack of inducing excess.

The three ages of Ibiza

ISLAND PARADISE: Undeveloped until the mid-1960s, the White Island was discovered by the Euro-chic and the rock aristocracy. Mick Jagger and the rest of the Lear Jet set basked in an exclusive sun while, elsewhere on the island, hippies set up camp and blew their minds.

THE PACKAGE YEARS: General Franco began forcible development of the island with concrete hotels and airports and it continued into the eighties. In 1986, 1.3 million tourists came to Ibiza and its neighbour Formentera, nearly half of whom were British. The once feudal fishing village of San Antonio was soon filled with chip shops and tattooed trippers. But the same influx brought with it UK club culture in a skeletal form. In the summer of 1987, DJs Paul Oakenfold, Danny Rampling and Nicky Holloway found that loud music and no sleep went well with a drug called Ecstasy.

CLUB MECCA: Then came the all-night raves. Out went the lager louts, in came the teenagers from the suburbs. Holiday operators, already running a network of cheap self-catering accommodation, artfully established youth ghettoes in resorts like San Antonio. The nineties have seen Ibiza become the mecca of serious clubbers. Between the end of June and mid-August more than a million people – half of whom are still British – come in search of two weeks of unchallenged hedonism. Dance magazines such as Ministry now print Ibiza pull-outs as UK clubbers migrate for the season. Manumission and Cream are among the more prominent clubs there; a trip to the island now costs around £750 for a week.

The Guardian 1 September 1998

Travel Matters © Carel Press

69

Peter Walker calls for a solution to the bedlam at tourist spots such as the Sistine Chapel

Judgement day for tourism

It is impossible to know how many millions of people have stood beneath the Sistine Chapel ceiling in the 485 years since it was painted by Michelangelo. So many millions, you think, that some people must have died there, on the spot, and perhaps even one or two were accidentally born there. But it's not the sort of place where you imagine anyone has ever been conceived. That, however, seemed to be the fixed intention of a young German couple I recently saw there, standing entwined directly under the *Expulsion from Eden*. And nobody turned a hair. That is because, in all the crush and the uproar and the shouts of rage from the Vatican guards trying to keep order, nobody noticed.

We are used to the idea that mass tourism degrades its objects of desire. We would all like to have wandered alone through, say, the Parthenon, or Stonehenge, or Chartres cathedral, but we accept that we cannot dismiss the crowd, because we are the crowd. In the Sistine last month, however,

Travel Matters © Carel Press

for the first time I saw a place where tourism, the destructive force, has reached critical mass, where the object of its attention is not just degraded but eclipsed, where there is almost no point in being there.

In the final approach to the Chapel, a recorded voice politely reminds visitors that the Chapel is consecrated and that photography is forbidden. But most people hardly hear that. After all, they are on the threshold of the sublime, which is no time to be listening to recorded messages. And there, suddenly, it is stretched out above you, the whole tale from *The Creation* to *The Last Judgement*, magnificently unfurled from one man's mind and magnificently cleaned by a Japanese television company. But there is only a minute or two to register this before other impressions crowd in: first, the noise. There are, perhaps, a thousand people there and they cannot help whispering, then talking; the laughing and the tumult rises and rises.

"Silenzio!" shouts an imposing figure, a tall man with a moustache, red face, wearing a police-like uniform. He is one of three guards on duty. For a short time, perhaps a minute, the noise subsides, then rises again.

"Silenzio!" a second one shouts, and "No photo!"

Flash! go the cameras. Flash! Flash!

"No photo!"

Flash, Flash, Flash! The guards rush this way and that, ejecting those they catch in the act. "No photo. You took photo. Out."

One man refuses to go quietly and answers back in a storm of Japanese. The two sides glare at each other, with clenched fists.

"Silenzio!" shouts a third guard across the room. "Silenzio!"

At first I thought that there was a language difficulty here, that the Japanese, in particular, did not understand that snapshots were forbidden. But watching more closely, I saw they were playing a cat-and-mouse game. Michelangelo is now immensely celebrated in non-Christian Japan and no one is satisfied with a mere postcard. They want him trapped and carried away in

"Silenzio!" a guard shouts, and "No photo!"
Flash! go the cameras. Flash! Flash!

their own Nikons and Minoltas. One young man beside me kept his camera hidden under his jacket. When the guards were busy elsewhere, he whipped it out: Flash!

"No photo, no photo, no photo," cried the moustachioed guard, pounding our way with a terrible look in his eye, not unlike Charon wielding a paddle on the wall above him. It is 10.30 in the morning and all the time more people are coming in, the tumult is rising again. The German couple are grazing and nibbling at each other's cheeks and neck. Her hands caress his buttocks. His hand rises to her breasts... At the far end of the Chapel, a group of teenage girls have taken over the seats along the side and are sitting on one another's knees, rocking up and down, chewing gum and biting the ends of their own hair, all of them pinkly aware of some French boys who are eyeing them up. One boy does a chimpanzee impression and gibbers.

"Our kids – if they use our toilet in the hotel – we go and use theirs," says an American voice in my ear. He was about 60 and talking to someone behind me. "I said to them: 'That's the way it is, kids. That's the way it's gonna be'."

That's the way it is, kids. That's the way it's gonna be. What I saw in the Sistine is now the way it is, wherever tourists gather. And as I said, we cannot dismiss the crowds. But this chapel is a special case. First, it is a single, confined space which was not designed for the great crowds which can be accommodated in the Pantheon, for instance, or the Parthenon, or be swallowed up in the gloom of a Gothic cathedral. Secondly, the principal attraction is a series of paintings of immense gravity and subtlety. The interpolation of pagan Sybils with Jewish prophets, for instance,

demonstrates that. But in the atmosphere of a fairground and a bun fight, it is impossible to get any sense of solemnity.

So what can be done? Ban amorous Germans? Ban French teenagers? Should tickets be sold a week ahead, to weed out the impulse visitor? One sadistic colleague suggests a compulsory hour-long lecture without slides, before entry. In Latin. If cameras are not to be used, then they should not be allowed into the Chapel: the temptation is clearly too great for the trigger-happy. Perhaps there should be sanctions sterner than shouting and the occasional ejection. After all the Vatican is a sovereign state and can make its own laws. The more I think of it, the more I like the idea – piles of confiscated cameras mounting in the guardroom, lines of convicted tourists hoeing the papal vegetable gardens under a merciless sun. Or should just the Chapel be shut up forever, like the caves of Lascaux?

Whatever the solution is, the bedlam below the Sistine roof surely can't go on. I couldn't help wondering what Michelangelo himself would have made of us all on that day. Among the 300-odd figures in the frescoes there are three crowd scenes, though they did not in the end give us much help. First, there are *The Elect*, whom we did not greatly resemble. Second, there are *The Damned*, and, well, we weren't that bad. Thirdly, there is *Mankind Escaping the Flood*. But that was not much use, either. In 1997, in the Sistine, mankind is the flood.

Independent on Sunday 17 August 1997

Prosperity and pollution find their way into a floating world

Guy Marks charts how the Uros Indians, living on man-made islands in the Peruvian Andes, have turned to tourism to give them a new sense of well-being

Puno, a town on the western shores of Lake Titicaca, 3,850 metres (12,630ft) above sea level in the Peruvian Andes, has a lot to answer for.

Pollution produced by its rapidly expanding population has for some time had a dramatic effect on a dwindling society of island-dwellers – the people of Uros who live on a series of man-made floating islands consisting of woven and compacted tortora reeds.

Some 120,000 people live in Puno. It is a dirty town with inadequate sewerage. The protected bay has become so infected that from a distance it looks like a well-manicured bowling green.

Closer inspection reveals that a thick carpet of duckweed, depriving everything below of light, grows over a greeny-brown soup of algae-infested water.

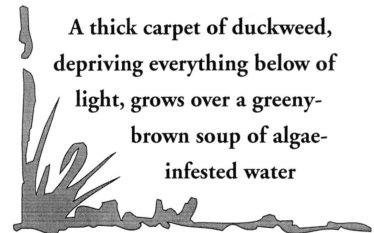

A thick carpet of duckweed, depriving everything below of light, grows over a greeny-brown soup of algae-infested water

The carpet is littered with floating plastic bottles and stretches right out to the start of the reed beds. Beyond the bay, however, it is relatively clean, fed by fresh riverine waters.

While the pollution has shown no recent signs of improvement, the fate of the islanders has nevertheless taken a radical turn for the better.

The Indians of the Uros islands survive on a diet of fish, and it was the eating from these polluted waters that was badly damaging their health.

The pollution became so severe that it killed all the fish in the bay about two years ago. Since then, the islanders have had to travel farther out from the lakeshore to find cleaner water.

This change came at a time when medical care, vaccinations and health education were all being brought to the islands, at the same time as they were experiencing an influx of tourism.

A hospital was built on Torani Pata, the main island, staffed by a full-time nurse Alicia Lerma Aguise, her assistant, and a regularly visiting doctor.

'We have eradicated cholera,' Alicia told me with great pride. Infant mortality is down so much that she considers it hardly exists any more.

She explained that occasionally children under the age of three accidentally become exposed to untreated water from around the islands. About 2 or 3 per cent may die, but the figure used to be 20 per cent. The

Uros floating reed islands, Lake Titicaca, Peru. A Uros Indian woman offers her wares to generate cash for vegetables, fruit and cereals.

population on the islands has grown – there are 680 families today compared with 400 in 1983. Alicia says this gives an estimated population of 3,400 – a far cry from the 300 quoted in many guidebooks.

Tourism has played a big part in this prosperity. On average throughout the year, about 30 to 40 people a day visit the islands out of curiosity about the extraordinary way the islanders exist on a matted bed of floating reeds.

A few years ago, the scene was pitiful – women sitting on the ground with meagre artisanal weavings, desperate for money and demanding tips for photographs.

Tourists were an intrusion, but the islanders have capitalised on this traffic. Each visitor has to pay an entrance fee, and art and craft stalls have sprung up on the main islands which promote tourism.

The pollution became so severe that it killed all the fish in the bay about two years ago

The crafts are brought mainly out from Puno, but they make no pretence about this. Trade is trade. Some bright spark noticed the tourists' interest in the traditional tortora reed boats and now short rides on these are offered for a few pence.

The money generated has enabled islanders to supplement their diets with potatoes, vegetables, fruit and cereals which they cannot grow on the reed islands. They have even bought solar panels and built a school.

Ironically, these shifts may have caused a dangerous dependence on tourism. For the moment, the changes overall are for the better.

Pollution from Puno, however, still remains as a priority to be tackled.

*Financial Times
27 February 1999*

Too much of a good thing?

Jean McNeil argues that eco-tourism may not be all it's cracked up to be

It's a dark night in rainy season Central America. I'm sitting upstairs in my attic room in a San José guesthouse listening to the percussive sound of rain on the tin roof. Downstairs in the guest house kitchen, fresh-faced visitors loaf, planning their next assaults on the 'jungle': 'I'm going to Tortuguero to see the turtles,' says Amy from New Hampshire, and everyone around the table coos.

Along with Belize, Costa Rica has become virtually synonymous with eco-tourism in Central America, and is widely regarded to be at the cutting edge of worldwide conservation strategy, an impressive feat for a small cash-strapped nation. So successful has it been at regenerating itself that other nations in this once-warring region are beginning to follow its example and seeking to improve their own economies through eco-tourist dollars. At the centre of Costa Rica's internationally applauded conservation effort is a complex system of National Parks and Wildlife Refuges, which cover a full 25 per cent of the country, making it the nation with the largest percentage of protected land in the Western hemisphere. These statistics are used with great effect to attract tourists. While an increasing number of visitors are arriving on simple, sun 'n' sea package tours, the vast majority still come primarily to see the country's remarkably varied tropical flora and fauna.

However, for years the country has been in danger of being overwhelmed by its own popularity; it attracts more than 700,000 visitors annually (the population of the country is only 3.5 million). And the important question to ask now is: how much damage is being caused by the feet of so many environmentally-friendly eco-tourists walking through the rainforests?

In the Manuel Antonio National Park on Costa Rica's Pacific Coast, visitors can walk the seaside trails, one of which circles the stunning Cathedral Point. As eco-tourism experiences go, it's a soft option, easily accessible and sandwiched between beautiful beaches. Here the squirrei monkeys, an endangered species, are so used to people that eco-tourists walking Manuel Antonio's trails complain about them behaving 'as if they were in a zoo', begging for food and being cheeky, or alternately hiding from the stress of having – on popular holidays like Easter, at least – literally hundreds of people trudge past their homes. Rangers at Manuel Antonio talk openly of the 'psychological pressure' large numbers of visitors put on some animals. And indeed, when the squirrel monkeys began to display symptoms of neurosis, officials took the decision to shut the park on Mondays, to give the animals a rest.

Monteverde and Santa Elena, two small farming communities high in the mountains of the Cordillera Central, are home to two reserves that together protect one of the last sizeable pristine pieces of cloudforest (high-altitude rainforest) in the Americas. In recent years increasing tourism has transformed the communities, and now flotillas of tourist buses rattle up and down the muddy roads connecting the towns to the reserves. In high season, the Monteverde administrators have had to impose a 100 visitor-a-day ceiling, in order to preserve the ecological integrity of the reserve, and both Santa Elena and Monteverde have taken the enlightened decision to resist paving a 40-kilometre stretch of road linking their communities with the Panamerican Highway, so that the journey takes too long for package tourists to be bussed up to the reserves then back down to their beach hotels on day-trips. Despite these measures, on busy days you'll still be fighting your way through gluts of safari-outfitted nature guides leading anoraked eco-tourists hell-bent on spotting a quetzal.

You could argue that an underdeveloped country in need of foreign currency can hardly complain about being too popular, especially when the type of tourism it has developed is so well-meaning. But it's arguable that Costa

When the squirrel monkeys began to display symptoms of neurosis, officials decided to shut the park on Mondays, to give the animals a rest.

Rica's environmental agenda stems less from environmental altruism, and more from a self-interested desire to make money from wealthy, first world eco-tourists who can console themselves that they are saving the environment. Meanwhile 38 per cent of Costa Rica's population live in poverty, without access to land. And while tourists now visit areas previously reserved only for scientific study, many tropical biologists have concluded that, in order to really preserve the rainforest, you would be better off staying at home and donating money to conservation organisations rather than travelling abroad to tramp through the forests and change local economies with the influx of your dollars.

In addition, the country's very assets threatened to turn Costa Rica into a science monoculture. The whole country has been roped into the eco-tourism cause: children are regularly taken on rainforest field-trips, and while it's true that their scientific and botanical knowledge is impressive, they many not be able to name the author of Don Quixote. 'Science is what this country has to offer,' one of my closest Costa Rican friends tells me. 'Science is where our future is. This country will produce great botanists and biologists, but I wonder if culture and the arts will be forgotten in this rush toward the scientific mind and the American dollar.'

Most Costa Ricans, however, especially those who work within the tourism and conservation industries, have a genuine belief that eco-tourism and conservation are the saving graces of their

country's national heritage (as well as the national coffers). Ask any National Park or private reserve administrator in Costa Rica about this and their response is usually the same: 'People are going to come anyway. You can't stop them. Our job is to make sure the tourism is managed properly.'

It's a delicate balance. There's no doubt that the financial success of eco-tourism has guaranteed the survival of many natural places, as you'll see if you look at the land not protected by reserves – for example, on the journey up from the Panamerican Highway through the lowlands, to Monteverde, which is now almost pure pastureland and clear-cut areas until you reach the green cool of the Monteverde mountains. Is this the alternative? To sell off the forest? At least with eco-tourism, say its champions, this way we can make it pay its way, and keep it standing.

I return to the musty, rainy season guesthouse to find that a group of kids from a Christian Midwestern college have arrived. The kids rise and shake my hand and call me ma'am. They're going to do a study tour, their teacher tells me, to find out more about 'God's nature'. They're coming here to find God in nature the way others come here to find themselves, or to receive some urgent if fuzzy message about the role of the Natural World in their lives. For them, I suppose, eco-tourism is neither a method of local people taking charge of the earning potential of their natural environments, nor is it a meaningless buzzword with a nice PR ring. It's spiritual tourism. It's a pilgrimage.

Jean McNeil is author of the Rough Guide to Costa Rica. She is Editorial Officer at Friends of the Earth.

Rough News Jan–Mar 1999

> ‘ **Travelling is like flirting with life. It's like saying: I would stay & love you, but I have to go, this is my station.** ’
>
> **Lisa St Aubin de Terán 1989**

the double curse

BY HILARY RUBINSTEIN

Travelling as a tourist in the third world is a double curse—for the poor host and the rich visitor

I HAVE ALWAYS believed, as a kind of truism, that foreign holidays—especially outside Europe and North America—are good for us, that they broaden our minds. Following a recent visit to India I have been having second thoughts. Travelling in the third world as a tourist from the west may have the opposite effect. Far from developing our understanding, it can highlight unwelcome truths about our character and reinforce our prejudices. More seriously, the role of the tourist in these parts of the world is inescapably patronising.

It was not my first visit to India. I had been there four or five times before, including six months in the RAF at the time of independence. I love Indian culture and food. I admire India's success in persevering with democracy when so many of its neighbours have long since lost their free press and the right to protest. I appreciate the ubiquitous good humour among the destitute. On a three-week holiday in Kerala and Rajasthan, I had many experiences to savour. But I have to admit that I was delighted to be home again—and won't mind if I don't return to India, at least for another ten years.

The first home truth I was forced to acknowledge was that I have no taste for Hinduism. I appreciate some of the outward manifestations of the religion—magnificent temples, fine carving and so on. But over the years I have suffered from the compelling need to try to understand the rudiments of Hindu mythology, and if possible, empathise with the Hindu faith. No longer. Dervla Murphy's book on her Keralan travels, *On a Shoestring to Coorg*, tells how her five-year-old daughter suddenly announced: "I think I'm too young to understand Hinduism. Will you explain it again when I'm eight?" I am still too young, and suspect that I will still be too young when I am 80. Is it a sign of maturity or philistinism that I have given up the struggle?

I deplore in myself a growing intolerance of beggars. Goodness knows, they have plenty to beg about—especially when you recall that many are in servitude to mafia-like gangs who require them to bring in a daily quota of rupees in return for the barest bed and board. All visitors from the west complain about that harassment. It must harm the tourist trade, but the Indian government have far more urgent matters to deal with: the continued rise in population; the widespread and growing corruption; the racial tension; the polarisation between the new rich and the growing masses who live below the poverty line. I sympathise with the enormity of these problems, but confess—with shame—to a hardening of the arteries of compassion when in India. I find myself losing my temper

---

I used to struggle to try to understand the rudiments of Hinduism. Is it a sign of maturity or philistinism that I have given up?

---

and shouting when beggars persist in their petty harassment.

The obligation to drive a hard bargain is another way in which Indian travel forces me into behaviour that I would rather avoid, especially on holiday. For the past 30 years I have earned my living as a literary agent, and I enjoy negotiating as good a deal as I can for my authors. But in India it is a different matter. All the guidebooks stress that you *must* bargain, that you would lose the respect of the vendor if you failed to challenge his outrageous demands. So I do. I flex my muscles, already in good trim from my occupational exercise, and I haggle like the rest, driving down the price for a pocket handkerchief, a postcard, a ride in a rickshaw, by a few rupees—a pittance by my standards, and a subsistence for him. It leaves a bad taste in my mouth.

Then there's the tipping. In Europe I hate the demeaning practice of tipping in restaurants. I regard it as absurd that you should pay extra for service in a ser-

vice industry and recall Bernard Levin's dictum that you never tip your equal. But in India you know that you are expected to tip on every possible occasion, so you do your best to equip yourself with plenty of small change and fumble to deliver what you hope is the right amount to every outstretched palm. And you feel demeaned again.

Travelling in India may not be doing much for my moral well-being but, apart from producing much-needed hard currency, what is my tourism doing for India? It would be different if I were in the country for professional, academic or business reasons, or visiting friends. But there is something intrinsically uncomfortable, even offensive, in the relation between rich visitors and poor hosts. If I am invited into a poor person's hovel, I become a voyeur—I cannot help it.

The tiny kingdom of Bhutan, northeast of Bengal, may have got the balance right. It charges $200 for a tourist visa, but then guides the tourists around the kingdom, thus reducing the unwanted fallout from visitors.

All mass tourism pollutes and benefits the host nation. But mass tourism in the poorer parts of the world tends to pollute much more. Worst of all, it is a double curse—to host and visitor alike. ∎

Prospect May 1999

'Do you believe all this global warming junk?'

The Spectator 16 January 1999

To serve and protect

The tourist industry does not want to kill the goose that lays the golden egg, argues **Roger Heape** of BA Holidays

Would you take an IQ test to see if you were bright enough to visit Venice? The wear and tear on the city and its treasures means some form of rationing for the future is necessary, but is this best done by only allowing access to those with an IQ to really appreciate its culture.

And what price a Pacific paradise? Anyone can stay at the Hotel Bora Bora provided they can afford $4,800 a night – just enough to keep numbers to the fortunate few.

Given that there will be 1.6 billion tourists roaming the world by the end of the century, spending $2,000 billion, it is difficult to disagree with the need to minimise the impact of tourism – but how and to what extent should this inhibit the tourist's right to roam?

Supporters of green tourism cite the ugly developments in Spain, building sites of the Turkish coast and the pollution of the sea in Pattaya. It appears that only low-volume tourism should be allowed. The irony is that green tourists go to some of the most sensitive sights on earth where environmental impacts may be just as severe. How many people can visit the Galapagos without affecting the ecological balance? And how should they be chosen – RSPB members?

Even low-volume tourism has unexpected side effects. Tooth decay in children in Nepal increased dramatically a decade ago – and the cause? Climbers on the Annapurna Trail handing out sweets.

What both the impact of mass tourism and eco tourism have in common is that the concept of carrying capacity is an issue. Putting it crudely, one frozen turd on Everest is not a problem, but several hundred are.

Close behind in attacking mass tourism are those who promote elitist tourism. Tourists are criticised for never seeing the 'real' country, never seeing the 'real' people, 'spoiling' destinations for others and 'crowding out' sites they want to visit in peace. They do not want picturesque sites to be destroyed, even though they are often, in reality, someone else's poverty.

Then, there are the cultural imperialists who highlight the social changes that come in the wake of tourism – the damage to communities and local crafts. Almost by definition, tourism is the big bad wolf. But do local people want to stay as they are? Why should they not enjoy the fruits of tourism? Tourism is in many places actually contributing to keeping alive or even reviving local traditions and crafts.

I am reminded of how easy it is to fall into the trap of forcing our world view on others. At a South Pacific Tourism Conference, I warned delegates against allowing tourism to spoil paradise. An islander got up and delivered a sharp retort: 'My great grandfather was a cannibal and your Scottish missionaries came and converted him to Christianity. The social changes that tourism will bring are small compared to that, and we can handle those ourselves.'

So how should the explosion of tourism be managed? The travel industry could set standards in the areas of energy reduction, waste disposal and water savings. It might also be able to suggest standards for planning and development. Many hotels now have environmental impact assessments before construction, recycle waste and encourage energy efficiency. And, of course, there is another major reason for good environmental practice in hotels. In the area of energy, it saves money and therefore increases profit.

Increasingly, tourist destinations do not want to kill the goose that lays the golden egg. St Lucia recently turned down a scheme to put a cable car and restaurant on top of its beautiful Pitons.

Consumer awareness is generally based on extra information in the brochures and educational eco-notes aiming to guide behaviour and highlight special points of environmental interest. For all its shortcomings, the travel industry is the best guarantee of the right to roam the globe and the future is about minimising the environmental impact of such roaming. A lot of little steps can, I believe, combine to build up to a major change in practices.

The Guardian 12 June 1999

TRAVEL NEEDN'T COST THE EARTH

You pay a lot for your exotic trips, but the land and the people pay more. By David Bellamy

When Walt Disney bought a patch of wetland in Orlando Florida, it was as barren as the dustbowls created by an earlier generation in the prairies of the mid-West. Florida was a prime example of the destruction of the natural landscape by the excesses of twentieth-century agriculture. The jobs had gone, the wildlife had disappeared and pollution was rife. Two-thirds of this area is now a nature reserve, perhaps a little manicured, but still a haven for the wildlife of the Everglades. On the other third, the Disney magic has created 45,000 well-paid jobs servicing the demands of millions of tourists.

You might be surprised, but I believe that Walt Disney World in Florida is an example of good practice in responsible tourism. It represents an example of sustainability as ethical as all those messages of good triumphing over evil which lie at the core of every classic Disney movie. If these messages were adopted more widely the world would indeed be a better place and the dream of sustainable tourism could come true.

Tourism is about travelling for pleasure and has grown into the world's number one industry. Yet for every one of us who enjoys the ritual of holiday travel, someone else at the bottom of the heap is paying a heavy price as their lifestyle is endangered.

There is growing recognition of the damage that modern economic development can cause. Take this quotation from the Herald Tribune: 'Economic globalisation is causing severe economic dislocation and social instability; technological changes have eliminated many more jobs than they have created; competition that is part-and-parcel of globalisation leads to winner-take-all situations, those who come out on top win big and the losers lose even bigger; higher profits no longer mean more job security and better wages... the backlash could turn into open political revolt and destabilise Western societies.' If these were the words of an ageing environmental campaigner you could perhaps be forgiven for taking little notice. But they were written by Klaus Schwab and Claude Smadja, representatives of the World Economic Forum which includes 1,000 of the largest global corporations.

It would seem that even those at the top of the pile are worried about the ethics of the world they have helped to create. I suspect that, like me, they probably like spending their holidays in exotic places as far from the madding crowd as possible.

After 10 years as chairperson of the now British Airways Tourism for Tomorrow Awards,

I am convinced that tourism may hold the key to the ethics of the twenty-first century and so save humankind from self destruction.

Those years have taught me many things... such as how important it is that more tourism money should be ploughed back into local economies rather than shipped offshore.

The 1993 award winner the Coral Cay Conservation, Belize, however, proved that retaining the money within a community isn't enough. It must be used to create local jobs and to provide training so that those jobs are not all at the bottom of the market. Education is vital – of the local people, the workforce and the tourists themselves, who must be taught the importance of the environment, of wildlife, local customs and traditional methods of land management.

Both the people and the wildlife (endangered and otherwise) need to be preserved, and a way of achieving this is by not building new resorts in areas of natural vegetation or pristine coastlines and landscapes. This was particularly evident when the 1996 winner the Taybet Zaman village resort in Jordan was selected.

But in some cases it may already be too late; the environment, people, culture and wildlife already polluted apparently beyond redemption.

Walt Disney World in Florida is an unlikely example of good practice in responsible tourism

One such case was Hanauma Bay, Hawaii (our 1997 winner), where a saturated tourism industry was threatened by its very success. To fight back, Hanauma Bay cut visitor numbers by almost two-thirds, and the industry survived.

Which inevitably begs the question, where can all those who couldn't get to Hanauma Bay (1.7 million in this case) go? And where can all the extra millions of new tourists go? There is obviously a need to open up new areas, and the focus for such developments should perhaps be on those places that have already been degraded, usually by inappropriate exploitation such as misjudged agriculture or logging.

But all action shouldn't be just reactive. The central region of Ghana (last year's award winner) showed how a proactive plan can work to produce a better, greener place. And I don't just mean patios and flowerpots; natural habitats have to be recreated for local animals and plants, and work carried out by local people using local crafts and sustainably produced materials wherever possible.

My question to young people would be: You plan your family holidays in a world of 10 billion people... how will you share the resource?

The Observer 27 June 1999

Politically incorrect places

Travel tips on visiting countries with unsavoury political regimes.
By Hilary Bradt

1) EXAMINE YOUR CONSCIENCE

If you are a political animal, you will probably disagree with me and feel that boycotting countries run by repressive regimes is the only moral way to express your opinions. You will be in good company. The charity Tourism Concern (Stapleton House, 277-281 Holloway Road, London N7 8HN) supports such boycotts, particularly to Burma. Check out their website (www.gn.apc.org/tourismconcern) and become a member so you can increase your understanding of the issues.

2) MEET THE PEOPLE

If you decide to go, you should make a conscious effort to talk to the local people. Carry a copy of a well-known English or American magazine or newspaper, and chances are that someone will want to practise their English on you. Steer them gently away from trying to sell you something, and ask about their lives (but avoid discussing politics unless they bring up the subject). Remember you are there to listen, not to impose your opinions. Resist the temptation to argue if their political views are different from yours—it is their country and they will have a greater knowledge of how it is run and how it affects their lives. If there is a language barrier, hire a guide/interpreter who can help you to meet the locals as well as providing their own insight. Expect to emerge sadder and wiser.

By visiting a country whose government we disapprove of, are we giving our tacit support to this government? Or are we just depriving innocent citizens of a chance to earn a living through tourism?

SUPPING WITH THE DEVIL

A HEATED DEBATE is currently taking place among members of the British Guild of Travel Writers on whether they should boycott Indonesia because of its government's repressive policies in East Timor. All travellers have weighed up this question: by visiting a country whose government we disapprove of, are we giving our tacit support to this government? Or are we just depriving innocent citizens of a chance to earn a living through tourism?

I know where I stand. I cannot be persuaded that sanctions or boycotts are effective; three decades of travel to the developing world have shown me again and again that the ordinary people want the chance to put their point of view to outsiders. The more repressive their government, the more they deserve to be heard.

I remember what led me to form this view. When planning our three-year odyssey through South America and Africa in the early 1970s, my friends assumed that as good liberals we would stay away from South Africa. I was inclined to agree with them, until we met an Australian couple who had lived there. It was their photos of Zulus and other tribal peoples which convinced us that there was another side to white-ruled South Africa, and we wanted to experience it for ourselves.

In South America, we learned that Chile's elected president, Salvador Allende, had been overthrown and a military government led by General Pinochet was now in power. The papers gave graphic accounts of the barbarous acts of the new regime. We continued anyway, and entered Chile only six weeks after the coup. We were utterly astonished to be approached time and again by the people of Santiago, who wanted to tell us how much they had suffered under Allende and how much they had welcomed the coup. We were deeply disturbed by this. We had been completely confident that we were at one with the people of Chile, that our outrage at what had happened would be shared by everyone we met, and here were citizens telling us with passion: "You must write to your friends, you must tell your newspapers, we are celebrating our new freedom!" As we hitchhiked down the length of Chile, everyone who stopped for us wanted to tell their story of suffering under the regime which we had admired from the safety of Europe and the Guardian newspaper.

After Chile, it was easy to go to South Africa and to hitchhike around the country listening to the people who lived there. Even an issue as clearly abhorrent as apartheid deserved an open mind. I learned to respect the Afrikaners, as well as deploring their actions. I learned to mistrust the smug English-speaking South Africans, despite their impeccable liberal credentials. I learned the true meaning of the word prejudice, and how not to pre-judge a nation by the actions of its leaders. I even learned that democracy, which we in the West hold up as the ideal form of government, may not be ideal for people of other cultures.

3) GIVE SOMETHING BACK

Make a point of supporting village economies by staying in small, locally-run hotels, eating street food or in local cafes, and buying handicrafts at a fair price (do you really need to bargain ferociously?). Decide on your policy towards beggars. By giving money, pens or sweets to children, you are doing nothing to improve their lives—but you may be keeping them out of school and teaching them how to get something for nothing. By giving to the elderly, on the other hand, you may be brightening one day in a miserable existence.

4) LONG-TERM AID

Seek out local charities that work with the very poor and offer long-term help (most Bradt Travel Guides list such organisations). A small donation can make a huge difference to these under-funded charities, or you can give them your medicines at the end of a trip. A visit to one of these charities can be the highlight of your trip and, with continuing support, will mean much more to you than an album full of photos. □

WEXAS Traveller Magazine
Winter 1999/2000

Spend spend spend

IT'S BEEN A BAD MORNING in the editor's office. First thing I read is a newspaper headline that screams at me 'Backpackers only want sex and fast food.'

Not that I want either at 9 a.m., but it's a shocking idea. Gone are the spiritual quests and questionable sandals of the hippy trail. It seems that today's backpackers are looking for pizzas instead of mantras. Their search is for shopping not salvation. Worse, they stand accused of blighting the globe with hostels full of washing-lines and cafés selling banana *lassi*. And this worries people whose travels are sensitive journeys in search of enlightenment.

Now the belief that travel has anything to do with enlightenment—rather than good old sun and fun—is worth pondering. It's largely the fault of that granddaddy of all backpackers, Jack Kerouac. Forty years ago he prophesied 'a rucksack revolution', in which youngsters would abandon the commercial values of our consumer society to find a higher wisdom on the byways of the world. Ever since then, generations of starry-eyed wanderers have believed that their travels should make themselves—and the lives they touched—spiritually richer.

So I find today's news perplexing. Has Jack been betrayed? Should we burn our batik shirts? Crucially, have I missed out on some spectacular hedonism? Here I've been, scribbling away about strange cultures and inspiring places, when I could have been enjoying dinner *à deux* with a backpackerette in the Macchu Pichu McDonald's—and never mind the view.

But then I remember the African sun, rising over the golden stone of the Namib Desert, while a tiny clipspringer— its eyes as black as velvet, its hide as taut as a supermodel's skin—lifted its delicate head from a waterhole and looked straight into my gaze for one endless, exquisite moment. I see a ragged grandfather in the mountains above Hanoi, who placed two precious eggs in my hands to thank me for visiting his bamboo shack, and the eggs were still warm from the chicken. I hear a friend in Udaipur who said: "You will learn more here than you will bring." And I can't believe that my fellow travellers are really neglecting such wonders.

I'm mulling over these little ironies when I open a press release on package tours to the foot of Everest. It stops me dead with its boast, that 'what took Sir Edmund Hilary 23 days in 1953 now takes 75 spectacular minutes in a helicopter.'

I wonder how Sir Edmund feels about that. I wouldn't blame him for wanting a helicopter himself, back in '53. But I don't suppose he likes what has happened to the world's highest mountain. It's been so heavily marketed, and become so easy to reach, that climbers now have to queue for the top. It can't feel very special up there any more.

The press release goes on to explain that the chopper-ride to Everest is only one stop on a round-the-globe tour that costs $22,000. For this, you get to see most of our world's wonders in just 21 days. How amazingly convenient.

And now the sobering thought hits me that we may reach a point when nowhere feels special anymore. When everywhere can be reached in 75 minutes or bought for $22,000, and burgers are served at the summit. If the free-spirited travellers have become mega-consumers on a binge, and the sacred places have become airstrips, then our planet and all that is in it will be just another convenience product, to be packaged, consumed and—eventually—garbaged.

Of course, it needn't happen. Each of us, from millionaire to backpacker, can choose the way we travel, the impact we make, the lessons we learn. At Machu Picchu, we can choose coca-tea instead of Coca-Cola.

Jonathan Lorie

*Wexas Traveller Magazine
Autumn 1999*

Craig Mitchell

Lurching into Lunch

Left: The island's shining beaches remain unspoilt – despite official efforts to promote tourism

Jack Barker watches the travel industry arriving on the tranquil shores of Madagascar. Pictures by the author

TWENTY YEARS AGO, STRUGGLING nations were told to grow coffee. The result was a world glut and a shaky slide in world prices. Today, tourism is the largest industry in the world, and the fastest way to bring foreign exchange into a developing economy. So the smart international agencies are pushing tourism as the new remedy for economic aches.

Madagascar has not got an economic ache so much as three missing limbs. Tourism is being asked to cure the problems of an eroding, deforested country that lives under a corrupt and repressive government in conditions of extreme poverty. To make the creation of a tourist boom even harder, scheduled flights are few, from South Africa or France, and internal communications barely function.

The European Union, however, is interested in promoting the region. They decided to fund a visit by 75 tour operators and journalists to see the island's highlights, make their own suggestions, and boost tourism generally. I was invited to represent a British newspaper.

Trade travellers are fussy and our party, culled from every country in Europe, constituted one of the largest and most demanding influxes the island has ever seen. Even the capital was stretched to find enough bedrooms. So we were split into five groups and sent to the island's furthest corners.

I headed down the Tsiribina River to the little visited west coast and the coastal town of Morandave. On the way, I met my fellow guests.

One was a small-scale British tour operator, three were Italians, and there was a firm clique of French. There was also a German representative of the International League for the Unemployed, who, speaking no French, spent most of the visit in a state of confusion. I met him as he

towered over hawkers and traders in a local market. "There's a lot of unemployment here," he growled through his beard. Each time he had eaten, he would fall asleep; on each occasion a French tour operator would record this achievement on the German's own camera.

Perhaps he wasn't used to eating so much. As we toured one of the world's most fascinating countries, we spent days in an insulated bubble where tour operators discussed margins and dual pricing structures with each other. Occasional sightings of waving locals, smoking bushfires and leaping lemurs were ignored, displaced by a constant desire to feast. The French tour operators regarded travel as a minor interruption in an orderly succession of meals. A few hours of modest activity came grinding to a halt every day at 12 for three hours of food and wine, from which no one had recovered by the pastis hour. But it was nice to see some EU money heading where it was needed, as official representatives signed away Madagascar's largest-ever restaurant bills.

FIRST STOP ON MY TOUR WAS MORANDAVE, a backwater paradise with a few accommodation problems. I stayed in a small hotel, disconcertingly sited among a horde of seaside bungalows, which showed no obvious signs of other facilities. "Where's the bar?" I asked, dusty on arrival. Slightly surprised, the receptionist replied, "It's in your room." How could I have failed to notice the fridge? As the hotel also lacked a restaurant, the official reception was arranged alfresco on the beach. The tablecloths were whipped by a brisk gale. "Is it always windy like this?" we asked. "Only in the evenings," came the reply.

Dinner was in a restaurant, courtesy of a potbellied Frenchman from Réunion, gold teeth glinting strangely in the candlelight, who explained how he'd spent the last seven years combining the best of French and Malagasy music. Then he launched two of his waiters onto a portable keyboard while our local guides rolled their eyes in agony at this travesty of their culture.

Hotel industry apart, Morandave was a charming town of smiles and greetings, dustily set against miles of white beach and sail-powered fishing canoes. The youth of the local fishing village turned up in an unofficial choir to sing traditional chanted music, strong, melodic and powerful. A village band, with ukuleles made from planks and broken-bucket drums, and instruments borrowed from the hotelier, performed real Malagasy music. Villagers ran in from the fields and pushed against every door and window to hear.

At this point, an Italian tour operator in our group remembered that he had left his briefcase, hat and trainers leaning against the outside of the hotel. As the pressing crowd of barefoot women and children dispersed, we found that these symbols of wealth had been left untouched.

There was plenty to see between lunches. Inland, the Tsingy is a wilderness of natural limestone cathedrals split by narrow alleys that look like a cross between the New York skyline and a cityscape from Star Wars. The surrounding plains are registered as a World Heritage site, thanks to their spectacular giant baobabs – thick-trunked bottle trees topped by stunted spiky crowns.

A local took me out to the bush to visit one of the oldest baobabs, thought to be 3,000 years old. Dense bush protected the base of a 25 foot-wide trunk, which towered hundreds of feet into the sunlight above and was crowned by the characteristic stubby, tortured branches. Small offerings and candles were lodged in a fold in the bark, and the tree was surrounded with healing platforms used by traditional doctors.

For the Malagasy, the spirit world is everywhere. Early efforts by British missionaries left a nominally Christian majority, but these new beliefs exist side by side with traditional ways of thinking – which invariably means talking to the dead. You see coffins on taxis, taking last tours of their favourite resorts; and for most tribes it is routine to dig ancestors up to ask for planning advice or just to have a party.

Unfortunately, we'd been invited to promote tourism, not enjoy it. All delegates were summoned to Madagascar's principal resort island, Nosy Be, to meet the country's ministers and officials in a formal conference. But a snap election had been called, which meant that most of our hosts were on the political slide.

In French, this didn't seem to matter. Doubts and ambiguities were hidden in a cloud of florid speeches which were devoid of real content. During a superbly dull discussion about road surfaces, I noticed, beyond the speaker, a scattering of Malagasy, walking far out across the flat sands where the full moon had dragged a low tide. Kicking off my shoes, I left the meeting and walked across to where the locals were foraging in shallow pools for shellfish. Across the flats, traditional songs were taken up and passed from one group to another in a timeless world. It was an idyllic moment. While the tour operators stayed in the conference hall, I wondered how much good the tourism business would bring to Madagascar.

On the flight back, I watched as an Italian photojournalist copied – word for word – pages of the Lonely Planet guidebook to publish alongside his pictures. Then I woke the German travel journalist in the next seat and asked him how he thought Madagascar's lurch into tourism would fare in his market. "I don't think it will," he said. "It is not Africa and it is not Asia. Besides, in Germany we don't know where it is."

It was the most encouraging news I'd heard all week.

Island paradise – but the children went on to eat the turtle

Wexas Traveller Magazine Autumn 1999

Returning the unacceptable PACKAGE

Visitors who spend most of their time and money in resort hotels will no longer be welcome in The Gambia, says Sophie Campbell

Hotels in The Gambia will no longer be able to offer all-inclusive holiday packages to foreign tourists from the beginning of November. In the first move of its kind in the world, the government of the West African country has placed a ban on packages which encourage holidaymakers to spend the great majority of their time and their money within a resort hotel and its grounds.

According to Saye Drameh, the tourism officer for the Gambian Tourist Board in London, the ban was prompted by 'the hotels which started offering all-inclusives last year without consulting the government: local people were worried about it, because some hotels were asking Gambians to pay to enter their premises'. The effect of the ban upon the local economy and culture is to be assessed; then, says Drameh, 'the government will finally decide if we want to have this type of tourism'.

British tour operators who offer holidays in The Gambia have switched clients already booked on all-inclusive packages to half or full-board, and in some cases have paid compensation. New brochures are being changed: in the latest published edition of Thomson's Faraway Shores brochure, for example, the Palma Rima hotel at Kololi Beach is now available full-board instead of all-inclusive, and at the same hotel First Choice now offers B&B with a possible upgrade to 'full board plus' (taking it perilously close to an all-inclusive package).

While organisations campaigning on behalf of developing countries applaud The Gambia's courageous action, the Federation of Tour Operators in Britain is less impressed. 'We regret any restriction on tour operators offering holidays which their consumers wish to book,' said a spokesman, 'and we feel that it is unfair when governments interfere in the free-market operation of tourism.' He added that a ban on all-inclusives did not mean that more money would filter down into the local

Local people were worried about it, because some hotels were asking Gambians to pay to enter

economy – because it would probably have the effect of persuading budget-conscious travellers looking for sun, sea, sand and sport to take their holidays elsewhere.

All-inclusive tourism – in which tour operators or hotels offer guests a complete holiday package of food, drink, entertainment and accommodation for a set price – has been controversial ever since it dramatically changed Caribbean tourism in the mid-1980's. The idea is not new: the French operator Club Mediterranée opened the first of its exotic, all-in 'villages' in the 1950s, and British holiday camps such as Butlins were an earlier version of the same thing. The difference today is one of scale.

Giant tour operators such as Thomson, Airtours and Cosmos send thousands of British holidaymakers to all-inclusive resorts each year. At Thomson, all-inclusives account for 65 per cent of its long-haul business (excluding Florida, which does not feature all-inclusive properties); for Airtours, the figure is 70 per cent. Long-haul specialist Kuoni sends 12 per cent of its clients to more than 50 all-inclusive hotels worldwide.

Other European operators, notably in Germany, Holland and Sweden, are equally keen.

As the market for all-inclusives has evolved, a lucrative short-haul sector has emerged in mature tourist destinations such as the Spanish 'Costas' or the Alps, offering packaged activity holidays for couples and families. But these destinations, already relatively wealthy, tend not to suffer from the same problems as in the developing world.

The controversy centres on the effect that all-inclusives have on host countries. A 1994 study of Jamaica's tourist industry found that such packages made the largest contribution to GDP, but that their impact on the economy was 'smaller per dollar of revenue than other accommodation subsectors.' In other words, all-inclusives made money, but not for local people. For the tour operator, the all-inclusive is a dream come true. The holiday-maker has paid for everything in advance usually in the operator's home country; with food and drink, entertainment and souvenir shops all on-site, there is little incentive to go elsewhere – except on the excursions arranged by the hotel. And catering is highly efficient when the number of diners can be predicted. For the consumer, too, predictability – of the cost of the holiday – is an advantage, as is high security and the guarantee of a multitude of distractions for the children.

Defenders of all-inclusives point out that construction companies, staff and food supplies must be obtained locally, and that having to provide so comprehensively for guests means that more service personnel and entertainers are needed than in conventional hotels. But detractors say that senior staff, furnishings and food products are often imported; wages for local employees are low; jobs are lost in the low season or when guest numbers fall; and profits are exported to foreign companies.

On the debit side, the lobby group Tourism Concern adds (in an edition of its newsletter devoted entirely to all-inclusives) that powerful tour operators and hotel chains can have a strong influence upon cash-strapped governments in developing countries, using their leverage to negotiate tough deals on wages, leases and food imports, which all adversely affect the local population. The resentment felt by local traders and residents at the glittering 'reverse ghettos' which have appeared in their midst, in which they are not welcome and from which they can make no money, is another focus for Tourism Concern.

'All-inclusive tourism goes hand-in-hand with the sort of attitude that says you don't want to be bothered by nasty foreigners or have to eat their food,' says Lara Marsh, a spokesperson for the organisation. 'It goes against the whole idea of travel as we might characterise it – as an adventure and a chance to meet people in other countries.'

For some destinations in the Caribbean, Africa and Asia, the choice could be between all-inclusive tourism or no tourism at all. In others, such as the Dominican Republic – which, for the travel business, is solely an all-inclusive destination – it is just one element of a mix: for guests from other countries, most of the island's hotels operate in a conventional

For some destinations in the Caribbean, Africa and Asia, the choice could be between all-inclusive tourism or no tourism at all

manner for bookings and billings. But in The Gambia, the all-inclusive business is tiny: it is less than a year old, and involves just three resort hotels featured by a handful of UK operators.

Had a high-profile destination, such as the Dominican Republic,

banned all-inclusive operations, the effect would have been dramatic; The Gambia is too small for its pioneering ban to be regarded as an important test case. And there are a few rumours that permission might still be given for up-market, all-inclusive developments that would add value to The Gambia as a destination. Ardy Sarge, chairman of the Gambian Hotels Association, says that local people would not object to all-inclusives as long as they were built away from the existing 'Tourist Development Area'.

Nevertheless, campaigners are happy with the The Gambia's decision – and its effects. 'The big test,' says Lara Marsh, 'was whether tour operators would pull out of the The Gambia completely. And they haven't.'

Sophie Campbell
© Traveller/ The Condé Nast Publications Ltd
November 1999

Of course, some of the sense of wonder and mystery disappears when you find that it's the local McDonald's.

Punch 21 January 1987

I SHOULD NEVER HAVE GONE

Barbara Toner

Craig Mitchell

THERE are holidays you shouldn't have had. I should never have gone to Cuba. Before I went to Cuba I was a kindly, left-leaning person, full of respect for the valiant island population clinging to its ideals despite the bullying of its humongous, bloated neighbour. Now I am proud to call myself bloated.

Of course I'm no longer liked. Everyone else who's been to Cuba loves it, even my brother-in-law, who would faint if he was called left-leaning. He said I would love it. He had such admiration for the schools, the hospitals, the safe streets, the deprivation but no poverty. 'What they want most of all is soap,' he said.

The important thing was to get there before Fidel fell off his perch and McDonald's moved in, to get there while it was still unspoilt. So I went. Two daughters had gone ahead of me to explore its glorious history and I thought what fun it would be, as sympathisers with the revolution, to visit the place together. In a way, it was. In an even bigger way, it wasn't. Sympathy wears thin in the face of what starts to feel too much like contempt for comfort.

I'm not saying that I, too, wouldn't feel contempt

Travel Matters © Carel Press

for foreigners who thought all I wanted was soap, but to be at the receiving end of it is ghastly. It turns you into a contemptible thing; in my case a bloated, mean woman with luxury-food items smeared all over her face, stinking of French perfume, dripping with dollars, telling everyone who wants more of them than I feel like giving to sod off.

I report this to my brother-in-law and it upsets him. He did business in Cuba for 20 years and loved the place so much he was on the first charter flight to Havana in 1994 as a tourist. He says maybe the best days have gone. Maybe the rot set in with his charter flight. Maybe it did.

The problem is the dual economy. Cubans who have only pesos to spend can buy just the bare essentials; Cubans with dollars can shop at the dollar shops and buy most things. Tourists arrive with dollars. The aim of the valiant island population is to extract as many dollars from the tourist as possible. And if I was earning $20 a month and knew tourists earned that much per hour at the very least, it would be my aim too. But sooner or later, in my case sooner, a tetchy tourist might start to feel ripped off. I was tetchy before I left Heathrow.

I had begun to feel ripped off when I booked two rooms at the Nacional, reputedly the best and most glamorous hotel in Havana. I used a specialist company where no one could say how much it would cost. The price they quoted went up, went down, went up, so I was thinking what was wrong with down? My brother-in-law said that I should have taken a package deal and he was right.

The cheaper flights to Havana are in seats that will accommodate just the one buttock, and, seven hours out of Paris, the lad next to me, with two medium buttocks, stopped moving. Even so, he was better off than I was. For the price I'd paid for my ticket, he was getting his flight plus ten days at a beach resort.

I had my first taste of communism on arrival. We landed at 8 pm, were still in the immigration hall at 10.30 and finally collected our luggage at 11.30. In the departure lounge, we were assailed by young men wanting to push our trolleys the ten yards to our taxis. I graciously tipped mine a couple of dollars because it was a full three days before I began to think, who cares if they're deprived?

A bog-standard room at the Nacional costs £60 per person per night—at least, that was the price I'd agreed in London— which is cheap by five-star standards, but this wasn't five-star. It has the most extravagant breakfast buffet ever, an attractive swimming-pool overlooked by an empty high-rise, and a very interesting Parisian cabaret. But my room had a broken chair in it and a cold-water tap that wouldn't turn. In reception was the rudest person I have ever encountered in reception anywhere, including the Vatican.

On the other hand, the sun shone, the old town was a short cab-ride away and only a totally churlish person would deny its charm. The buildings are spectacular, gorgeous colonial piles falling tragically to ruin, and the squares are bustling, though they are bustling mainly with tourists wandering in and out of shops and restaurants almost exclusively for them.

We visited the Museum of the Revolution, which is moving for the first ten rooms, the Museum of Colonial Art which has quite nice furniture in it, Mass at the cathedral, where the singing sounded exquisitely like the soundtrack from *Evita*, as well as many art galleries. One night we went dancing. We travelled to a desolate place where local girls were waiting outside for tourist boys to take them in. The dancing didn't start for two hours. We decided not to wait and the man at the door chased us to our taxi. I guess we looked rich.

The aim of the valiant island population is to extract as many dollars from the tourist as possible

Most nights we had dinner and then came back to the hotel. Food in Havana is usually awful and not especially cheap. The best is served in the licensed private houses which charge tourists about £25 a head though a Cuban friend of my daughters said locals pay far less.

That's the problem. It's not so bad being approached in the street by people asking for dollars. It happens every day in London. What gets to you is the knowledge that you're being charged what the Cubans think they can get you to pay. Havana taxi-drivers use a standard rate but what they want more than anything is for you to hire them for long trips out of town. We took a trip to the botanical gardens, a 45-minute drive away. It was a morning's journey, but the driver's greatest concern was hanging on to us over lunch. We said it wasn't possible. He said he guessed he wouldn't be eating then. I didn't care. How mean was that?

The point is, when you think you're being fleeced, you stop enjoying what there is to enjoy, like the music and the art. After a week, I couldn't take another musician staring into my eyes while he played yet another melody and tried to flog me his CD.

I remain full of respect for Cuba's education, its hospitals and its safe streets, but how long will they last when the population's so fed up with deprivation?

Two maids at the Nacional wrote to me at the end of my stay hoping I was satisfied with them. I tipped the first and gave the second a packet of sanitary towels. She didn't look grateful. I felt grotesque. I should never have gone.

Barbara Toner is a columnist for the *Mail on Sunday*.

The Spectator 29 January 2000

WHEN TERROR RETURNS IN TINY DETAIL

Photo: Magnum

The horrifying murders in Uganda last week (the slaughter of eight tourists, kidnapped by political rebels while on a gorilla-spotting safari) took me vividly back to when I was kidnapped two years ago, while back-packing with a friend through Guatemala.

We were travelling on a dirt track through dense jungle when our minibus was held up at gunpoint by two camouflaged men. The six other passengers were all European tourists in their twenties. My friend and I were the only Britons.

After being marched off into the jungle, we were made to lie face down on the ground like rows of sardines.

THIS IS POOR OLD SUE, HIT IN THE LEG BY AN AK47...

Colin Whele

The Spectator 20 February 1999

Four other gunmen were waiting in the clearing, armed with machine guns and machetes. It was then that I thought I would die. Some people screamed and cried, while others like me stayed silent, paralysed with fear. Luckily, our captors had loot rather than murder in mind. They searched each of us in turn, forcing us to hand over our money, then rifled our luggage, taking everything from toothpaste and Tampax to clothes and Nike trainers. Finally they urinated all over us and our belongings before leaving us to barefoot it back to our bus.

Strangely it all seems rather surreal to me now. The nightmares have subsided and I try hard never to dwell on the event. But last week's terrible news brought back every detail, right down to the ants crawling over my face.

Sarah Angus
North Kensington, London
Mail on Sunday 7 March 1999

When going overseas becomes a journey fraught with danger

GETTING THERE
BY JEFF MILLS

AN ENGLISH acquaintance of mine who used to be based in Rio de Janeiro never took the same route from his home to his office. He told his driver to vary it every day in case one of the many local villains worked out there was a pattern and could attack and rob him in his car or break into his house while he was known to be out.

Perhaps he had spent too long as an expatriate in Brazil, but he had plenty more horror stories as he emphasised to visiting friends and colleagues the need to be extra vigilant. He would often illustrate the need for caution by relating stories of the latest methods adopted by local gangsters to relieve foreigners of any cash and valuables they were foolish enough to carry with them.

One of these involved attacks on cars stopped at traffic lights. Drivers often left the windows open for some fresh air. The gangsters would lob a live snake through the driver's window. The drivers did what any sensible person would do – opened the door and ran – whereupon the gangsters would simply jump in and drive off.

I was going to say this may be an extreme example of the kind of things that can happen to people travelling abroad, but after recent horrifying events in a number of overseas countries I am not so sure.

Tourists visiting Luxor in Egypt in November 1997 were doing nothing to provoke the terrorist attack which left many dead or seriously wounded; those who are robbed in some European and North American cities are innocent victims who are doing nothing more than boosting the economies of the countries they are visiting.

The tourists abducted from their camps in the Bwindi National Park in Uganda by Hutu rebels last weekend, eight of whom, including four Britons were killed, had been visiting the country to view wildlife. Instead they seem to have become political pawns in a particularly macabre guerrilla war.

The travel advice unit of the UK Foreign & Commonwealth Office was last week publishing a list of no fewer than 17 countries or states to which it advises Britons not to travel at all and a further 11 which should be avoided unless you have essential business there.

> **The tourists became pawns in a macabre guerrilla war**

The no-go areas effectively make a large proportion of the globe off-limits. On it are Afghanistan, Algeria, Burundi, the Democratic Republic of the Congo, the Republic of the Congo, the Chechen Republic, Eritrea, Iraq, Jammu and Kashmir in India, Sierra Leone, Somalia, north and east Sri Lanka, Sudan, Tajikistan, Western Sahara, Yemen and Kosovo in the Federal Republic of Yugoslavia.

The Foreign Office also advises Britons against all but essential travel to Angola, the Central African Republic, Djibouti, Ethiopia, Guinea Bissau, Liberia, Montserrat, north-east Albania, Rwanda, south-east Turkey and the Serbia and Montenegro areas of Yugoslavia.

In the case of Uganda, the Foreign Office has advised against all travel to the country's border areas with Rwanda and the Democratic Republic of the Congo and reminds Britons who really do have to visit the country that from 1 March they have needed visas.

These are bleak days for travellers who like to get off the beaten track. Their choice of destinations is becoming more limited by the day. These are also difficult times for tour operators specialising in arranging holidays to many far-flung exotic destinations, none of whom would dream of operating tours to areas effectively blacked by the Foreign Office.

As a spokeswoman for one prominent company pointed out last week, if there is trouble in one small African country, for example, it affects people's wish to travel to any part of the continent, even if the area they were planning to visit has never had trouble of any kind. Demand for holidays to India last year was down 84% year-on-year, though a very small part of the country (Jammu and Kashmir) has been affected by unrest.

Strangely, however, the same operator reports that demand for holidays to Egypt, which dropped away to virtually nothing after the Luxor massacre, is back at normal levels.

It seems that Britons are more resilient than many people may imagine – or have very short memories.

Sunday Business 7 March 1999

Broader horizons, wider minds

What's wrong with 'risky' foreign travel? asks Lyn Hughes, editor of Wanderlust magazine

What is the most common cause of death or injury when you are travelling abroad? Terrorism? Violent assault? No. It is far and away the good old road accident. Pranging the hired car or falling off a holiday moped is a much more likely occurrence than getting mugged, caught up in a riot or eaten by a lion. And yet, time and time again, we see any venture abroad that goes beyond a sun, sea and sand package holiday labelled as something dangerous.

This was brought home at the end of December when the news broke about some Brits being taken hostage in Yemen. The phone in my office at *Wanderlust* magazine started ringing at nine sharp in the morning. 'Know anything about Yemen? Can you do a quick interview?' By lunchtime we had a TV crew squeezed in among our desks and several radio interviews under the belt.

No details had been given about the hostages at that point and so the media was jumping to its own conclusions, painting a picture of young thrill-seekers who got a kick out of visiting dangerous places. 'Do they go to these places looking for danger?' 'What advice would you give their parents?' There was genuine shock when it was revealed that these hostages were middle aged and middle class.

Meanwhile, as the media feeding frenzy got underway, a real-life tragedy was unfolding. When the news came through that several of the hostages had been killed, many members of the media turned hostile towards anything and anybody connected with 'adventure' travel.

A Radio 5 presenter asked why I took 'wild risks' by going to destinations further than Benidorm: 'Are you mad?' Another asked, 'Don't you think it's irresponsible of your magazine to run articles on dangerous countries?'.

I tried to explain that British tourists have been killed in Florida, the Caribbean and Australia in the past few years, yet none had been killed in Yemen in the same period. Anyway, who is to say which is a dangerous country? The advice the Foreign Office was giving out on Yemen prior to this incident was very realistic, warning of kidnappings. On the other hand, tour operators got very frustrated recently at the over-cautious official warnings that went out about the risks facing British people travelling to Chile (during the General Pinochet case)

and China (after NATO bombed its embassy in Belgrade).

When the IRA was bombing the British mainland, did we warn tourists not to visit us? There would have been outrage if the USA had declared that the UK was unsafe and Americans were not to visit.

Then there is Egypt, another Middle Eastern country where tourists have been killed. And yet we have short memories. Most tour operators who go there report a resurgence of interest, with numbers of visitors almost back to the levels before the Luxor massacre in November 1997. Just a couple of weeks after that dreadful massacre, I was on a live travel show when a viewer rang in and expressed her disappointment at her dream trip having been cancelled. She wanted to know whether there were any companies still doing trips to Egypt that she could switch to. This was no danger-seeker, but a typical package holidaymaker.

Perhaps the media reaction stems from ignorance. In the case of a country that has had little attention over here (I bet a lot of journalists would rush to their atlases to find Yemen) it is immediately categorised as being full of savages. But the most annoying thing to come out of the barrage of nonsense spoken both before and after the events in Yemen was the claim that people like me go travelling in

search of danger. Nothing could be further from the truth. Serious, responsible travellers do their homework, weigh up the risks, and take rational decisions.

People travel to places like Yemen because of a desire to experience a foreign culture, see the exotic, and to taste the unknown. This was certainly true of the group kidnapped, who were intelligent, educated, well-travelled people. They were well aware of the political and cultural situation before they went to Yemen. They were travelling with one of the most respected and experienced tour companies around.

What didn't get reported was that several British groups that were out there at the time of the kidnapping chose not to cut their trips short. Indeed, one of my readers who was out there rang up to say that Yemen was 'truly amazing', and that her group had felt 'completely safe'. She said she felt desperately sorry for Yemen and how the tragedy would hit its budding tourist industry.

Sadly, shortly after the Yemen incident there was the awful tragedy in Bwindi National Park, Uganda, where eight tourists were killed by Rwandan rebels in March. It seemed to confirm the view of some members of the media that the travel industry is callously sending unwitting tourists out to dangerous corners of the world. Again, they were doing travellers a disservice. Thousands of people a year have been travelling safely to the border parks of Uganda to see the last few mountain gorillas living in the wild. To trek through muddy paths for several hours, and then spend an hour in the company of our nearest relatives is an unforgettable experience. It is one that intelligent, caring people will hopefully want to continue to have—they are probably the gorilla's only chance of survival.

Castigating travellers for pursuing their interests in foreign lands is ridiculous. Of course an element of risk comes with all travelling, but by just getting out of bed in the morning we are opening ourselves to risk. Travelling can be rather scary, but not because of any physical dangers. Culture shock and new experiences conspire to challenge us abroad. But that is how it should be, and that's why an intelligent person loves travelling. Anybody who believes that travellers just do it for the risk should get out a bit more—preferably overseas. ●

LM Magazine July/August 1999
Website www.informinc.co.uk

DIY Britons break free of package holiday hell

Most Britons seeking their place in the summer sun have had to endure package holiday hell: a patronising tour rep, lukewarm sangría at the welcoming party and dawn trips to be at the airport five hours before the flight.

But the current generation has had enough. Fed up with foreign trips regimented by reps with irritating patter, record numbers of holidaymakers are turning their backs on the packages that promised nothing abroad would be 'too foreign'.

A new survey shows that, for the first time since mass tourism began in the Sixties, more Brits are now organising their own breaks than taking the packages offered by tour companies.

'British holidaymakers are a lot more sophisticated now,' said leisure consultant Anne Bourgeois. 'The baby-boomers who went travelling a lot when they were young know exactly what they want and where they want to go. They are able to pick their own accommodation and book their flights to achieve the flexibility that they believe packages can't offer.'

Cheaper air travel to a growing list of destinations as well as easier access to popular continental places through the Channel Tunnel have boosted the spirit of independence.

'Low-cost, no-frills airlines have opened up cities to many more people and the consumer is becoming very good at shopping around to find the best bargains,' Bourgeois said.

Media company manager David Greenwood, 30, is typical of the new breed. His parents were among the first generation of package tourists who travelled to one-time favourites such as Rimini, Italy, on propeller-driven planes from Biggin Hill, Kent.

His idea of a break is very different. 'I took a holiday to Goa with a package company on a charter flight because it seemed easy and it was cheap. The flight was a nightmare with everybody crushed in.

'The hotel was okay – it was one of the least package-like. The only activity I got involved with was the welcome drink,

but it was just an embarrassing attempt to sell us all the tours they were running. I worked out we could get to the market for the equivalent of 6p on the local bus. They were charging something like £9, and you had to go exactly when it suited them with a whole bunch of people I had no interest in getting to know.'

Independent travel is no longer associated only with backpacking and far-off destinations, the survey by market research firm Mintel shows. Top of the free-thinking traveller's list of destinations is France, followed by Spain – aided by accessibility and the strong pound.

But self-drive holidays in the United States and flight-only bookings to European cities are also soaring in popularity.

Thousands of small hotels now post their details on the Web, so more travellers are e-mailing hotel owners directly.

The language barrier is less frightening in print than over the telephone, researchers found. Jennifer Cox, the Radio 1 travel presenter and spokeswoman for *Lonely Planet* guides, said the Internet is driving independent travel rapidly forward. 'We get more than three million hits a day on our website. Package holidays were based on the assumption that you didn't know how to do it yourself, but now technology means there

is well-packaged information which is readily accessible and interactive.'

Short, city breaks are more popular than ever, and these also tend to be booked independently. Twice as many people will take a short break to the Continent this year as did in 1994, when the Channel Tunnel opened. There was a further boost when the air industry was opened up to greater competition in 1997.

Domestic holidays are less popular than they were six years ago, and only the taste for weekend breaks is sustaining the UK home market.

Although the statistics show that there are twice as many holidays taken at home than abroad, consumers spend more lavishly on foreign trips. The average spent per UK holiday is £161, compared to £400 on an overseas trip, not including the travel to and from the destination.

'More people go abroad for their main holiday because we are just too expensive in Britain,' said Robert Unsworth, editor of *The Good Guide to Britain*.

'We still persist in charging per person instead of per room and offer worse value than probably anywhere else in the world. But short breaks are a different story. People want the minimum hassle, to go somewhere relaxed with something nice to do. Britain is a good place for that.'

Foreign breaks rather than domestic holidays are fuelling the record popularity of getting away. Mintel estimates that 100 million holidays will be taken this year – two million more than in 1999 when the total spending on breaks was £23.5 billion. Spending this year is forecast to reach £24.3 billion.

Sarah Ryle

The Observer 12 March 2000

The top travel innovations

Frank Barrett on the holiday pioneers who changed the lives of ordinary people

The 20th Century has seen many travel innovations: factor 24 sun cream, Y Viva España, suitcases with wheels, the bikini...The Mail on Sunday's Travel Editor chooses his (more serious) top five.

The modern shape of tourist business effectively dates from the day in the early fifties when Walt Disney took his daughters to a California funfair and recoiled in disgust at the tawdry stalls and litter-strewn surroundings.

A man who ran a business which demanded the most painstaking standards of production was entitled to wonder why similar standards didn't apply equally to amusement parks and Disney decided to create one where families would enjoy the highest levels of quality in a safe, controlled environment.

While friends and colleagues privately derided the idea of the creator of Mickey Mouse and Snow White becoming the proprietor of a glorified funfair, Disney bought a plot of land in Anaheim, California, and built his park called, with an impressive lack of modesty, Disneyland.

Its opening confirmed the slowly growing realisation that tourism had evolved into something quite different from the concept pioneered by Thomas Cook more than 100 years before. It was no longer simply the sum total of combining transport arrangements with accommodation bookings – holidays had become a branch of showbusiness.

Travel companies, like film-makers, are effectively selling a dream – though in the case of certain tour operators this would probably have more the properties of a nightmare!

By creating his own 'world', Disney had taken the first steps towards a concept of 'controlled delivery' through which holiday suppliers endeavour to control every element of a package to ensure total satisfaction.

But arguably his biggest impact was in sparing no labour or expense in ensuring the highest standards.

Before Disney, holidays were seen as 'fun' things in which quality of service or product were reckoned to be of no consequence. While people were in a holiday mood anything would do for them.

Disney realised that the exact opposite was true: people deserved the best during their precious holiday time. The most complete realisation of his dream is to be found at the four theme parks which make up Walt Disney World in Orlando, Florida.

Laker

Like Disney, Freddie Laker with his Laker Airways was a man who had a vision and asked: 'Why not?'

Why not offer a low-cost trans-Atlantic airline service with the bare minimum of on-board facilities – something like a flying train.

Until the mid-seventies, air travel was still largely the preserve of the wealthy. Laker talked about the 'forgotten man', the ordinary person who was just as entitled to travel by plane.

He proposed to call his service Skytrain. To achieve his dream he took on the airline establishment and national governments.

British Airways executives treated his ideas with contempt, arguing that cutting the air fare to New York wouldn't mean more people would fly – they said the same people would go on flying, operators would simply be left with decimated revenues. But, with extraordinary bulldog spirit, Laker fought and fought until finally he was given permission for his 'turn up and take off' Skytrain.

From the day it was launched, the travel business was never the same again. The cheap fare genie was out of the bottle. His rapid success inspired the American government to usher in a new age of deregulated airlines.

Freddie got a knighthood for his troubles, but the airline establishment never forgave him. When the pound plunged against the dollar, Sir Freddie proved vulnerable to a concerted attack from his competitors, who quickly seized the opportunity to shoot him out of the skies.

Laker always claimed foul play and he was eventually justified when BA subsequently had to hand him a multi-million pound compensation payment.

Sir Freddie has never entirely left the airline business – Laker Airways flew the Atlantic again a few years ago in a temporary but very admirable display of dogged defiance. Richard Branson picked up the Laker mantle (a fact which he happily acknowledged when he named one of his first 747s the Spirit of Sir Freddie).

Holiday Inn

While Disney was busy revolutionising the amusement park business, a man called Kemmons Wilson established a new concept in the hotel industry – the Holiday Inn.

After family trips driving across America during which his family had to stay in shoddy overpriced motels, Kemmons Wilson was sure there would be a demand for a new style of accommodation.

So on 1 August 1952, in Memphis, Tennessee, he opened the first Holiday Inn in what proved to be a fast-growing chain (within five years there were 100).

Children were allowed to stay free, there were swimming pools, air conditioning, free cots, in-room telephones and televisions, ice machines and plenty of free parking.

While Holiday Inn later became identified with the bland American homogenisation of service and standards, the people who criticised it had clearly forgotten how awful things had been before.

HORIZON

The year 2000 marks the 50th anniversary of the charter flight-inclusive package holiday invented in its modern form by Horizon Holidays.

Its creator was Vladimir Raitz, now 77, he's still energetic – he helped to launch a programme of cigar holidays to Cuba a few months ago. A summer holiday on the island of Corsica in 1949 derailed him from a career in journalism into setting up his own holiday company. He took the unprecedented step of specially chartering a plane to take his clients to a campsite on the island.

In doing so he effectively changed the face of the entire British holiday. Families who once saw Bognor Regis as the limit of their travel ambitions quickly became familiar with Spain, Greece and Portugal.

The Dutch-devised Center-Parcs revolutionised the British short break just as much as Disney re-invented the amusement park.

In 1967 sports shop owner Piet Derksen realised his dream of offering a holiday 'in a villa in the forest' with his first park of 30 villas with an outdoor swimming pool in southern Holland.

When it made its first appearance in the UK a decade ago, in Sherwood Forest for the first time the British were offered a weather-proof holiday.

There was the fine swimming pool in the signature subscription-tropical dome – and there was a huge array of top-class sporting facilities and high-quality self-catering accommodation.

What Sir Billy Butlin had done for the working classes with his holiday camps in the Forties and Fifties, CenterParcs has done for the middle classes in the Nineties.

CenterParcs achieved the almost unthinkable: it has made Britain fashionable once more as a holiday destination.

The Mail on Sunday 26 December 1999

The traditional
seaside

The death of the traditional British seaside holiday has been greatly exaggerated. The saucy postcard image is alive and well in the cheery surroundings of Skegness. Look no further than Torquay if you fancy continental brio without the language barrier. And if you want to mix highbrow nightlife with daytime donkey rides, head for Scarborough. At the height of the summer season, the Holiday Which? team set out for nine big resorts around the UK to check out what they have to offer.

The State of the Seaside

'Vacancy' signs were a common sight around the seafront streets of Blackpool, Great Yarmouth, Rhyl and the like. Bad weather didn't help a trend that's seen the number of visitors staying and spending money at British resorts falling since the 1970s. The annual exodus to the nearest kiss-me-quick resort has largely gone the way of one-piece bathing suits for men, afternoon tea dances, and knotted hankies as sunbathing headgear. Sadly, battleaxe boarding house landladies (and landlords), unseasonably bad weather, and the practice of emptying raw sewage into the water where we swim are still much in evidence. We do still like to be beside the seaside, but it's much more likely to be beside the Mediterranean these days.

As a result, many traditional British resorts are in a spiral of decline that has left many of the major attractions around the coastline in a depressing state of disrepair. The overriding impression of our traditional resorts is one of ageing infrastructure, tired ideas and low-quality accommodation. The Pavilion at Ayr is boarded up and largely derelict. Birnbeck Pier at Weston-super-Mare (like so many of our Victorian seaside follies) is a ruin, while stretches of the seafront villas at Rhyl look terribly run down and decrepit. Just 22 of the 1,000 places to stay in *The Which? Hotel Guide* are in major seaside resorts.

Extract from a report in *Which? July 1999*

Is the traditional seaside holiday a thing of the past?

Yes, James Ledward
Editor, Brighton Impact

No, Roger Dawson, Hotelier, Rhyl

Dear Roger
The picture painted by last week's *Holiday Which?* report of British seaside resorts in a 'spiral of decline' is, sadly, an accurate one. It reflects the British tourism industry's failure to identify and tackle the reasons why people have stopped taking their holidays in this country.

Many British people have been choosing foreign destinations for their holidays since the 1970s, but it was Margaret Thatcher urging the masses to aspire to something better that was the final nail in the coffin of so many British resorts. Value for money was her battle-cry – and too many British resorts provided anything but.

The idea that, ten years on, Thatcher's children might be satisfied with a family holiday in Rhyl – described in the report as 'down-at-heel and depressing' – is hard to comprehend, when their parents have experienced the high standards and quality offered by many European resorts.

The only British seaside resorts that will survive are those such as Blackpool, Bournemouth and Brighton, which have realised that the dream of the 'family package holiday' lives no longer, and have developed a much more liberal marketing strategy.
Yours,
James Ledward

Dear James
Were you aware that only 20m people in the UK have ever flown in an aeroplane – and that of the foreign holidays sold each year, a great proportion are due to people taking two holidays or more? The vast majority of people in the UK take their holidays on home ground.

With more leisure time and more choice when to take that time, the trend is to take shorter breaks more often.

Most 'value for money' foreign holidays exploit local populations with the excuse 'Well, what would they do without tourism?' If that's what you want, it's your choice. Foreign holidays haven't replaced the traditional British holiday. They run alongside them and, yes, the choice should be there.

Most of Britain's city coastal resorts have accepted changes to satisfy specific lifestyles. Some have lost direction, due to lack of leadership, and some have found it easier to roll over and die. But many couples do come to Rhyl. The area also boasts castles and gardens, stately homes, country houses, waterfalls, canals and historical sites. There's a proliferation of nightlife that is open as late as allowed by the laws of this country.

James, if priorities for your family include burning all day and drinking all night, off you go abroad – because the variety round here would exhaust you.
Yours,
Roger

The Guardian 10 July 1999

SEA, SUN AND SNOBBERY

JUST WHAT IS IT with backpackers and people who consider their globetrotting so very alternative? They really do believe they're trekking uncharted territory, don't they? Armed with their Rough Guides, a change of undies and determined to return with boring tales of getting to grips with some authentic culture or distant civilisation as yet untarnished by the tourist industry.

Last year my mate Bob expressed his intention of joining this legion of superior and supercilious adventurers. As someone whose continental travels had been restricted thus far to an occasional 14 nights on the Costa Brava accompanied by his parents, Bob's planned push bike ride around Europe came as a shock.

While considering what to pack in his panniers, he began developing those annoying personality traits exhibited by every would-be globetrotter. Bob was not going on holiday – he was 'travelling'. And why stop at Europe? With a bit of work along the way and a back wind he'd be crossing borders for some months to come.

Within a week Bob had returned to these shores – the sad excuse being worn wheel bearings and a total lack of ateliers de réparations de bicyclette this side of the Champagne-Ardenne. But even now, unable to halt his evolution into a peripatetic snob he insists that the world is his oyster, and like many others is casting his eye towards far flung exotic destinations – although he plans getting there without the helpful assistance of Thomsons or Thomas Cook.

That old Monty Python sketch springs to mind with Eric Idle showing disdain for anyone who, like me, enjoys their holidays to be of the packaged variety 'What's the point of going abroad if you're just another tourist carted around in buses surrounded by sweaty mindless oafs from Kettering and Coventry in their cloth caps and their cardigans and their transistor radios and their Sunday Mirrors, complaining about the tea – "Oh they don't make it properly here, do they, not like at home".'

The point is that we do like to be mindless when we get away from it all, we do want tour operators to sort the full itinerary and every arrangement for us. We're determined to relax and escape the stresses and pressures of home – why anyone would reject the comfort and well ordered nature of an ABTA protected vacation in favour of the trials and tribulations that plague independent travel is beyond me.

Importantly the package holiday is no longer restricted to dismayed tourists being herded into the half built Hotel Miramar on the Costa Del Sol, although that's still there if you want it. Let's stop being snobs right now – 18 million people are predicted to head overseas on package holidays next year. And with good reason: you can get package deals to climb Mount Everest, to swan around Argentina's 22 enviro-friendly national parks, to ride on a skidoo in Iceland. Literally every corner of the globe, any activity you can think of and any size of wallet has a package deal to suit.

Of course what most of us want and what repulses the few is a good dose of sun and fun. Francis Bacon once said that 'travel, in the younger sort, is part of education'. He was patently talking about the orgiastic delights of Club 18-30 or 2wentys.

Imagine this: You wake up with the mother of all hangovers and it all starts to come back. You'd spent the day indulging in games that involved licking ice cream out of her belly button, you danced until daylight with the occasional break for some sex in the surf, you were flirting with the reps, they were flirting with you. You even learned some interesting new watersports. Then you look around, realise you're in the wrong hotel and there's still 13 days left.

Now is there something wrong with me? I can't think of anything I'd rather be doing. And if that makes me the worst kind of alcohol-abusing, projectile-vomiting, randy, rampant Brit abroad then so be it.

Backpacking? It's for wusses. Inter-railing? For trainspotters. You want real adventure? It's the package holiday you need.

The Big Issue 7 February 2000

THE WORLD'S MOST DANGEROUS PLACES

They are the world's least likely tourist destinations.
Wealthy travellers bored with annual trips to Barbados or Tuscany are looking for more adventurous holidays and turning to war-zones and the most dangerous countries on earth for excitement.

With itineraries including Algeria, Chechnya, Afghanistan and Iraq, these independent terror tours are for those who want an adrenaline rush rather than a sun-tan. Many of the most dangerous countries, such as Iraq and Algeria, boast stunning historical sites dating back thousands of years, alongside the kidnappings, murders, bombings and civil insurrection which have made them infamous.

Although trips to hazardous areas require meticulous planning and often cost many thousands of dollars, tour operators and embassies report a marked increase in the numbers of tourists visiting danger zones. Embassies report increased visa applications while travel insurance companies are excluding war-zones and trouble-spots from their global travel insurance policies.

Visitors to unusual parts of the world are increasing dramatically. Last year the Antarctic received 15,000 holidaymakers, five times as many as in 1991, while in Cambodia, a nation still wracked by guerrilla attacks and regular fighting, western tourists flock to the serene temples at Angkor Wat. Trips to see the

wreck of the Titanic will soon be available at nearly $30,000 a head, while two Japanese businessmen have even paid to go into space on a Russian rocket. Many of the new breed of independent travellers have done the normal tourist trail to countries such as India and China. Now, according to Philip Haines, a British traveller who has organised recent trips to Iraq, they want something different.

Trips to see the wreck of the Titanic will soon be available at nearly $30,000 a head

---

For nearly $2,000 Haines has been offering tourists a Royal Jordanian Air flight to Amman and a four-wheel drive journey across the Iraqi border (an obligatory Aids test as you cross is $50). Highlights of the tour include a boat trip on the Basra marshes, an outing to what the Iraqis claim is the site of the Garden of Eden, and a whirlwind trip around Baghdad while staying at the city's four-star Al Rashid hotel, from where the BBC's John Simpson watched Cruise missiles fly past his window during the Gulf War. Haines planned to take a small party of tourists to Iraq this Easter until the small matter of Western air-strikes intervened.

Among those who booked tickets are two solicitors, an archaeologist and a policewoman. John, one of the solicitors, refuses to reveal his surname because he is keeping his holiday destination secret from his employers, who only know he is taking a short break.

Chantal Van de Cruys, an adventurous Belgian traveller, returned from a short trip to Iraq only last week. She has fallen in love with the country and its history since her first visit in 1994, and regularly takes parties of up to 15 tourists in to see historical and archaeological sights. 'It's a magnificent place, the cradle of civilisation,' said Cruys, who teaches psychology near Antwerp and has travelled throughout Africa and the Middle East. 'Most of the people who go in with me have travelled throughout the world and are interested in Iraq's long history.'

Cruys plans to return to Iraq in April, but thrill-seekers who want to go it alone without a tour-guide must turn to an eclectic guide-book titled *The World's Most Dangerous Places*, which has just been re-published for the third time and can be bought in English across Europe.

The book offers practical advice for those needing a late-night taxi in Baghdad (after 10pm there is a surcharge), or wanting groceries in Afghanistan (shops open at 8am but many close on Wednesday and Friday). Robert Young Pelton, the book's Canadian author, and his team of writers research their book by traversing the globe. They have the stories to prove it: the author, a Fellow of the Royal Geographical Society, has broken Americans out of jail in Colombia, lived with the Dogon people in the Sahel, been attacked by PKK rebels in Turkey and survived a plane crash in the central highlands of Kalimantan.

According to Pelton his book is an attempt to educate people to be aware of danger, not to glamorise the violence of war-zones. However *The World's Most Dangerous Places* is lauded as a Bible by adventure-seekers, and the

tourists seems to be the buzz they get from danger. John McBride, for example, is a 53-year-old former British soldier who spends 11 months of the year working for $200 a week as a council dustman in Glasgow, and one month in the world's hell-holes.

Last year saw McBride in Rwanda, just months after the country's borders had reopened following genocide and civil war; he admits some people think he is 'sick or totally insane'. He now rates Rwanda as the most nerve-wracking of all the 84 countries he has visited, while other experiences he proudly relates include being held-up at gunpoint in Afghanistan and the time he was questioned for hours by trigger-happy young soldiers in El Salvador who believed he was a CIA spy. Other terror-tourists have not been so lucky. An American businessman travelling as a tourist in the Chechen capital, Grozny, disappeared without trace early last year, and a Frenchman travelling by foot in Chechnya is believed to have been blown-up during a Russian artillery bombardment of rebel positions.

While respectable travel agents would never put their clients in danger, some have come in for heavy criticism for their willingness to take people into danger-zones. An Italian

travel agency has admitted, for example, that it organised holidays for tourists on the front-line between warring armies in the former Yugoslavia. Armed guards were hired to protect the mainly wealthy Italians on the trip, all of whom were required to sign disclaimers absolving the agents of any blame should they be shot, maimed or killed.

Other tour operators have gone further, and there have been persistent rumours of German companies organising sniping holidays in the former Yugoslavia during the last months of the bitter civil war. Some German tourists were being taken into the hills near Sarajevo by Serbian soldiers and shown the best spots from which to hit civilians in the town below. Other German tourists are believed to have actively participated and taken a few pot-shots of their own.

A Frenchman travelling by foot in Chechnya is believed to have been blown-up during a Russian artillery bombardment of rebel positions

first two editions sold out within weeks of landing on shop shelves. The book rates several nations as being genuine five star Hells on Earth: including Algeria, Somalia, Sierra Leone and Burundi. Pelton believes the market for travel to dangerous parts of the world has increased partly because of the falling price of air-tickets. 'Nowadays $1,200 will take you anywhere, that's what makes adventure travel the in thing,' he said.

The main motivation for terror-

There have been persistent rumours of German companies organising sniping holidays in the former Yugoslavia

Perhaps the motivation for dangerous trips can be found in the otherwise normal lives led by the travellers. While many are wealthy and independent, most are like Chris Savage, 39, and his wife Sue, who hope to travel to Iraq with Philip Haines. 'We always seek out adventure holidays,' said Chris. 'I'm a chartered accountant but I wanted to be a lion tamer.'

Simon Reeve

When rage is part of the package

Photo: Phil Houghton

According to a psychologist, if you put mice in the same conditions as air passengers they'd eat each other.

By Nick Hopkins

Captain John Austin boarded flight AIH 71 from Gatwick to Jamaica last Sunday believing his 30 years experience as a pilot had prepared him for anything.

Seven hours later when he radioed to make a forced landing in Norfolk, Virginia, and pleaded for police back-up, he had changed his mind.

The journey had been the most terrifying of his career and his 13-strong crew – all experienced stewards and stewardesses – were in a state of shock.

Members of the Working Group on Disruptive Passengers gathered for the first time the following morning at the Department of Transport's headquarters in Westminster. The meeting was given unexpected piquancy by the antics of the "Airtours 12" and the headlines they had secured with their alleged behaviour.

The members, including representatives from the Civil Aviation Authority, the British Air Transport Association, and the Association of Chief Police Officers, were discussing air rage. But instead of action to prevent further outrages and punishments for offenders, they were battling over the definition of the phenomenon and how best to collect data from airlines for research purposes.

Capt Austin, meanwhile, was writing his log in the Caribbean, describing in detail how his Boeing 767 and its 325 passengers were put in jeopardy at 35,000 ft.

At one point, eight stewards and stewardesses were grappling with the unruly passengers, raising the prospect that the crew might lose control of the cabin as the plane travelled across the Atlantic at almost 600 mph.

The industry, it seems, has a lot of catching up to do before it comes to terms with the problem.

Alcohol is a cause, but psychologists also point to the change in travel culture over the last 20 years – the availability of cheap flights and high density seating – as important factors.

"Human beings were not built to be huddled in confined spaces for extended periods of time. If you put mice in the same crowded environment that we put passengers, they'd eat each other," said Helen

Muir, a professor of aerospace psychology and a chartered psychologist.

Alcohol undoubtedly contributed to last week's furore, though there are two different versions of the story.

According to the 12 passengers ordered off – six men and six women from Ireland and south London – they were enjoying a boozy "sing song". "We're victims," said Elizabeth O'Driscoll, aged 22, when she arrived back at Gatwick on Thursday morning. "Sure, a few drinks were taken by some of us, but this thing has been blown out of all proportion."

Capt Austin's report, which may be used as evidence for charges of endangering the aircraft under the Air Navigation Order, suggests otherwise. The group's high spirits turned to abuse before the headsets for the in-flight entertainment had been handed out, he claims.

They demanded alcohol, though the crew suspected they were already drunk. When the trolley arrived quarter of an hour later, they were offered only one drink. "They became very demanding and the crew refused to serve them."

Capt Austin's report describes how the 12, who were sitting together at the back of the 767, started drinking their supplies of duty free beer, rum and cocktails, despite warnings that this is illegal.

"They went up and down the aisles, approaching other passengers to ask them to buy drinks on their behalf... in a confined space like that, it was very difficult for people to say no," the report says.

This continued for five hours despite pleas from the crew, who noted other passengers were getting "extremely aggravated and upset". One eventually cracked, throwing a glass of beer over 35-year-old Miles Connor when he asked if he would buy him a drink.

"All hell broke loose," the report says. "Eight or nine members of the crew had to intervene to get things under control."

Fighting between the seats spilled out into the aisle. "The situation was completely out of control."

Capt Austin tried to restore order by issuing several warnings, but finally announced that he was diverting the plane to Norfolk.

At that point, the group calmed down and started to clear up the mess they had caused. The crew said the 12 passengers had been "acting like animals" and that the passengers, "had been extremely frightened".

The 12 were marched off the plane at Norfolk by FBI agents.

"It is very scary when people start behaving like that," said one Airtours source. "The crew can't call the police. They can't run away. They've got to deal with it. This wasn't a good old fashioned Irish sing-song, and flying isn't the same as going on a road trip to Blackpool."

Looking at the figures, it is easy to sympathise with the airlines that insist air rage, though disturbing, is more of a media invention than an ever present danger. With the number of people flying – 85 million were carried by UK airlines alone in 1997 – it is inevitable that some flights will carry troublemakers.

The Civil Aviation Authority, which defines air rage as behaviour which endangers an aircraft, recorded 62 incidents in 1997 and 63 in 1998. This is statistically insignificant when you consider the number of flights involved – more than 1.5 million each year. Virgin Atlantic said it had only four incidents of air rage last year.

A study published this month by Robert Bor, a professor of psychology at London's City University, is more worrying.

He reports that British Airways, the world's largest international carrier, recorded 266 incidents of disruptive, as opposed to dangerous, behaviour on board aircraft in the 12 months before the end of last March – a 400 per cent increase since 1995. American Airlines reported a 200 per cent increase in passenger interference with flight attendant duties between 1994 and 1995. There were 450 incidents on board United Airlines flights in 1997.

The effects of alcohol on behaviour are well known, but according to Dr Muir, there are other sources of stress in the cabin which could lead to disruptive behaviour.

Sudden changes in barometric pressure, an increase in carbon dioxide levels and long periods of humidity can trigger violent mood swings.

Howard Davies, of the British Air Transport Association – which represents nearly all of the country's airlines – denies the industry plays down the problem, or that it should consider banning alcohol. "The majority of passengers who have a drink behave well."

"Why should we deny them the pleasure of a glass of white during a meal just because of a few thugs?"

Dr Muir accepts his logic, but adds: "It's quite possible that we'll have an air rage catastrophe soon.

"In some ways, it is surprising it hasn't happened already."

The Guardian 6 February 1999

Sure, it was just a little *craic* in the sky

says Simon Hoggart

YOU'RE ON A TRANSATLANTIC flight, say to the West Indies. You're anxious for a nap, and you're desperate for the children to get some sleep, because otherwise they'll ruin the first few days of the holiday. But you can't, because the passengers from hell are keeping up a barrage of noise two rows away.

It happened to me once. A whole rugby team got on at Heathrow, some actually carrying – unchallenged – pint pots of lager onto the BA 747. By the time we were halfway to Seattle they were roaming the plane pissed as rats, crashing into people with their lumpish rugby players' bodies, singing *There Are Seagulls Round The Lighthouse* and spilling drinks on little old ladies and Americans who, contrary to what you might think, are the most docile passengers in the world.

So I have every sympathy with the people on the Airtours flight to Jamaica who had to put up with 12 drunken Irish people singing at the top of their voices. Airtours will also have done itself a lot of good, even if the travellers successfully sue them: 'We dump troublemakers and make them find their own way home' is a slogan that would make any reasonable person want to book a holiday with them.

No doubt it's a cultural thing. If you fly very rarely, you could well imagine that a plane is just a long thin pub, and that getting wellied, singing and fighting are appropriate behaviour. But there are other social lessons to be learned. One of the

evicted group said that they hadn't done anything wrong, but were just having 'a good old-fashioned Irish sing-song', as if that was explanation enough.

All nations have myths about themselves. These are important; they help bind a country together. We used to believe we were top nation, and now the Americans know they are. The French think of themselves as the most sophisticated. And the Irish have always believed they were the Most Loveable People On God's Green Earth, a view that has survived the IRA, the Real IRA, and some of the most corrupt politicians in Europe. The chap who talked about the sing-song was, I am sure, genuinely baffled: how could the airline have confused loveable Oirishness, the craic at 35,000ft, with unacceptable behaviour?

The Spectator 31 July 1999

The Guardian 6 February 1999

Passenger jailed for attack on crew

Jackie Brown

A DRUNKEN British passenger who punched two airline crew while a plane was landing at Singapore's Changi airport was yesterday starting a one-year jail sentence.

Richard Weeden, 34, from London, was also fined 1,000 Singapore dollars (£375) for the attack on a British Airways Boeing 747 London-bound flight from Perth. Australia.

The plane carrying 400 passengers and 16 crew was about to touch down in Singapore en route to Britain when the attack took place on Monday.

Weeden pleaded guilty to four charges of causing injury and being drunk on an aircraft when he appeared in a Singapore district court on Wednesday. The court was told that he had been drinking heavily on the plane and went to sit on the stairs of its upper deck shortly before the aircraft landed at Changi.

He refused to return to his seat when asked by stewards, shouting and punching one in the chest and nose. Another steward was hit before Weeden was subdued and handcuffed by cabin crew after touchdown. He was taken away by airport security.

A British High Commission official said Weeden had been visited by consular staff.

A spokeswoman for British Airways welcomed the sentence, saying that one of the stewards had suffered a hairline fracture to his nose.

"We will not tolerate air rage in any shape or form. We are extremely pleased with this direction and hope such a ruling will deter other passengers. We are pleased that the Singapore authorities also take this seriously and we thank them for their assistance."

Press Association
The Scotsman
14 August 1999

PLANE INSANE

Why is everybody obsessed with 'air rage'?
asks Brendon Craigie

Never has flying off on holiday been so easy, so cheap...and so scary. These days you are quite likely, it seems, to fall foul of a fellow passenger afflicted by 'air rage'.

In February, air rage was transformed from a tabloid soundbite into an official category of offensive behaviour, when the Civil Aviation Authority (CAA), the airlines and the police started collecting uniform data on it for the first time. Home secretary Jack Straw and his Tory predecessor Michael Howard have both looked into legislation to deal with it, while airlines around the world have been searching for new ways to keep passengers under control. Japan's national airline, JAL, now gives permission for its staff to tie up and gag unruly customers, and it has become standard practice for most major airlines to carry handcuffs on passenger planes.

Headline stories about drunken, out-of-control passengers causing havoc in the air have helped to inflame anxiety about air rage. In 1998 British Airways terrified the media by reporting a 400 percent increase in violent incidents over three years. Yet as the CAA's head of flight operations, Captain Mike Vivian, explains, 'the percentage of unruly passengers is still tiny - last year UK airlines carried 85 million passengers, while only 100 individuals caused trouble'. That is one troublesome character for every 850 000 passengers - hardly an epidemic of in-flight violence. (On the ground, by way of comparison, there is approximately one murder for every 100 000 British citizens.)

The high-profile demands for tougher action against those accused of air rage seem way out of proportion to the relatively undramatic statistics. Virgin Atlantic reported only four incidents of air rage last year, yet Richard Branson has called on airlines and holiday companies worldwide 'to ground for life anybody who acts violently. It needs draconian measures like that to make people think twice before they behave in that manner on planes'. Transport minister John Reid admits that air rage attacks are 'extremely rare', yet insists that the government takes the problem 'very seriously'.

There have also been many calls to ban alcohol on planes, since drunkenness is a common explanation for the relative increase in air rage incidents. Yet according to the CAA, 'alcohol is not the major cause of airborne disruption - accounting for only 25 percent of incidents'. A more realistic assessment might conclude that many of the passenger incidents reported today are actually provoked by the airlines' ban on smoking. As figures released by the British Air Transport Association claimed, of 1000 incidents where staff or passengers were threatened or abused in 1998, 60 percent were linked to smoking bans.

Perhaps the relative increase in air rage is better explained by the new role allotted to airline staff by employers.

Flight attendants were once considered to have glamorous careers. Now they are more like a cross between a tea-lady, a door-to-door salesman, and a security guard. British Airways (BA) trains its flight attendants in a three-step method of dealing with difficult passengers, depending on what state they are in. The response escalates from soothing conversation, to the issue of a 'yellow card' warning of possible arrest upon landing, to the forcible use of handcuffs. A BA spokesperson assured the Daily Telegraph that handcuffing by its smiling special constables was 'rare': 'Of the 41 million people who flew on the airline last year, only 20 were subjected to it.'

BA and Virgin championed recent arrests of air rage suspects in the name of protecting their staff from duress, while airlines and unions representing pilots and flight attendants have played a key role in encouraging prosecution of aggressive passengers. New York Times journalist Laurence Zuckerman

The Spectator 7 November 1998

'AIR RAGE PROVIDES A PERFECT PANIC FOR OUR AGORAPHOBIC, CLAUSTROPHOBIC, MISTRUSTFUL SOCIETY'

notes how 'as part of the stepped-up campaigns, many airlines now encourage employees to report incidents, offering them legal advice and paid leave to testify in court. Before, staff were discouraged from filing complaints because the airlines were wary of offending customers'.

With staff trained like sniffer dogs to be ever-alert to air rage and to report incidents to the police, the growing statistics are not all that surprising. And when fear of air rage is as widespread as it has become today, staff are likely to become even more sensitive to the potential terror up above.

But why are the rest of us so concerned about a handful of airborne rowdies? Separate the facts from the headlines, and it becomes clear that the growing awareness of air rage far outstrips the rise in actual incidents. Concern about air rage resonates so widely because it provides a perfect panic for our agoraphobic, claustrophobic, mistrustful society. The fear of being caught on a plane, in a confined space from which there is no escape, sitting right up close to drunk, out-of-control people you have never seen before, can invoke a powerful sense of 'stranger danger' in the sky.

However many people are grumpy after a long, uncomfortable, nicotine-free flight, the fact is that very few try to take it out on the airline staff or passengers. And in any case, with the flight attendants cowering in the cockpit and jumping at shadows, passengers are going to find it even harder to get drunk.

LM Magazine July/August 1999
Website www.informinc.co.uk

They'll drive you crazy...

ALL Italian drivers are mad – one sweeping racial generalisation I will defend.

I know, for instance, that not all Scots are mean nor all Welsh wonderful singers (although my wife is a Scot and very mean as it happens and I'm Welsh and, to tell you the truth, sing like a nightingale).

But Italians are – to a man and woman – certifiably bats when they put themselves behind a steering wheel.

For the past week I've been driving in Tuscany and stand bemused at the level of passion which Italians bring to the simple process of, say, driving to the shops.

If they consider that you are holding them up, they sit on your bumper about two inches back with their engine screaming like reverse thrust on Concorde and wait for five yards of clear road in order to complete an overtaking manoeuvre of terrifying recklessness.

On the motorway, anybody doing under 500mph in the fast lane is considered some sort of mental incompetent who has to be harassed using every available option short of machine gun fire. They're not bad drivers – they don't dither at roundabouts and clearly signal their intentions at junctions – it's just that they're, well, mad.

But anyone who has ever taken their car across the Channel has discovered that even in France, road users have bizarre habits.

I remember in the early Sixties, the first time that I went abroad with my parents. We were about 10 minutes from Dunkirk when we saw our first Frenchman relieving himself at the side of the road (little did we then realise that this appalling sight would become as familiar to us in France as the Citroen 2CV).

My mother had a grandstand view of a swarthy man in a beret and asked: 'Why is he peering over that hedge?' she mused. Well, she was almost right. Unabashed, the peeing Pierre offered us a cheery smile.

There was no clue about how to respond in our motoring guide which concentrated on the hazards of not observing bizarre French laws which gave priority to traffic from the right – even tumbrils emerging from farm tracks and on roundabouts which meant you had to give way to traffic joining the roundabout.

A lot of these ancient customs have since lapsed – in theory, at least. In practice the French tend to do what they want (in or out of the car!)

Abroad they do things differently. The latest edition of the RAC's Motoring In Europe guide reminds us just how differently.

Back home we suffer clampers and tow-away – but in Rome the penalty for illegal parking can be a jail sentence. Next step: arm the traffic wardens!

DID you know that in Gibraltar the maximum speed limit is 25mph or that in Finland all vehicles must use their headlights at all times outside built-up areas?

In Portugal if you can't produce vehicle documents, your car may be confiscated. You also face an on-the-spot fine if you do not carry your passport when driving.

There's an idea for John Prescott to cut down on the number of road users: make them carry their passports. Given the present troubles of the Passport Office the roads will be clear in weeks...

Frank Barrett
The Mail on Sunday
22 August 1999

Road rage alarm

FOUR out of five men feel uneasy while driving, because they fear 'road rage', a new survey by bus firm Arriva reveals.

Nearly a third carry potential weapons in the car, such as crowbars, repellent sprays or knives. The survey also found that 42% of women carry personal alarms.

AA Members Magazine
Winter 2000

It makes me so angry!
The things about fellow passengers that annoy passengers.

AIR		RAIL	
Noisy and loud people	15%	Mobile phones & conversations	23%
Excess hand baggage	8%	Noisy & loud people	12%
Being inconsiderate	6%	Smokers/smoking	4%
Invading my space	5%	Overcrowding	2%
Reclining in their seat	4%	Personal stereos	2%
Smokers/smoking	4%	Creating mess & litter	2%
Children/babies	3%	Taking up too much room or	
Wanting to talk	3%	spreading across the table	2%
BO & other smells	2%	Being inconsiderate	2%
Being late for take off	2%	Feet on seats	1%
		Double seat hogging	1%

Holiday Rage
Top 10 irritations for UK holiday makers. Figures show percentage of total complaints.

Standard of accommodation	41.4%
Accommodation charges	10.8%
Building work	7.7%
Overseas reps	5.1%
Flight change	3.6%
Flight delays	3.1%
Food	2.7%
Car hire	2.4%
Pre-bookable flights	2.2%
Overbooking	1.4%

Co-op Travelcare, 2000, Figures for summer 99

We don't want all those grumpy tourists in London

We hate them and, if we are honest, the only reason we let them in is that we want their money, says Philip Hensher

LONDON MOSTLY likes foreigners, but dislikes tourists. Many, perhaps most, of the people who now live in London weren't born there; they came for a job, liked what they saw, and stayed. London is generally welcoming to anyone who wants to make their life there, and on any Tube journey you can overhear conversations in half a dozen languages. The city is full of people who were born in Italy, Australia or Uzbekistan, but found their way there and discovered, to their surprise, that they had become Londoners. London, in general, likes foreigners.

But it hates tourists. People who come for a week and see nothing; who eat in the Angus Steak House and complain about English food; who come in November and complain about the weather. Norwegians who don't take off their gigantic rucksacks in the Tube and then call the English rude – we hate them. Italians who, under the impression that no one in the world understands their language, talk loudly about how many blacks there are – we hate them, too. Australians who go on about how crowded and noisy it is – they just haven't seen the point.

Most of all, London just can't stick the sort of visitor who doesn't seem to realise that he isn't in Kansas anymore. A week or two ago, I was queuing in the bank between two gargantuan American matrons, who were trying to change some money. One asked for 'two hundred dollars'. The cashier reached for a wad of American dollars. 'No,' the woman said. 'I mean, like, two hundred English dollars.' 'English dollars,' the cashier repeated, raising an eyebrow with the faintest ironic inflection. Yes, we hate them and, if

we are honest, the only reason we let them into a country they have no interest in is this: we want their money.

So three cheers for the new *Lonely Planet Guide* to London, which has just been published. It's apparently been written by some idiot who should never be allowed to pass judgement on anywhere livelier than Saffron Walden. London is terribly dirty. Londoners are a lot of litterbugs – their word. There is dog shit everywhere. Everything is very expensive. The food is 'over-refined' – a novel complaint. Rock Circus is no good.

Well, cor chase my Aunt Fanny round a mulberry bush. Is that the best they can do? Frankly, I'm worried that this won't be enough to persuade tourists that they would be better off going on holiday to Singapore, where the air conditioning works, the streets are clean, and you can spend your holiday gazing at MTV. I do see that they are trying very hard to put people off, even to the point of telling lies – the guide's claim that bars in London all close at 11pm will come as news to anyone who has been to Soho in the past five years. It's interesting, too, that the guide complains about the rudeness and self-absorption of Londoners when the truth is that tourists, too,

have a bit of a duty to behave politely. The woman in charge of the *Lonely Planet Guide* was saying yesterday that Londoners 'come across as aggressive if you go up the wrong side of the escalator on the Tube'. Most people will wonder who is being ruder here; the habitual Tube user or the idiot who ignores signs and blocks the escalator.

The truth is that London is the most welcoming big city in the world. It is the most successfully multicultural city in Europe. It is expensive, as everyone knows, but that, in part, is because it's so good at creating wealth on dozens of different fronts. It's got a livelier literary, musical and artistic society than any other city in the world. The food is fine. It's really very safe and best of all, unlike every other city in the world, it isn't remotely snobbish.

That sounds unlikely, so ingrained is the common perception. But London doesn't belong to England; it belongs to Londoners. And there is no distinction to be made between 'true' Londoners and people who have adopted the city. Parisians are snooty about people who weren't born 'intra muros'; New Yorkers go on and on about the 'bridge and tunnel crowd'. London just leaves you to get on with it. It is, frankly, the only place to live; it makes everywhere else seem provincial.

These kind of complaints have two effects, I can't help thinking. And anyone who loves London will welcome both of them. First, there will be the sort of hick who reads it, and decides to go somewhere duller, and safer. But then there's someone like you or I, who reads that London is dirty, rude, and awash with money and thinks only one thing: that sounds like my sort of town.

The Independent 11 February 2000
© *Philip Hensher 2000, first published in The Independent*

'Polluted' Blackpool all at sea

Manchester Evening News Syndication

BY GEOFF MEADE

BRITAIN was last night told to clean-up the sea at Blackpool — or face heavy fines.

The famous resort and nearby Southport are under fire for failing to come up to European Commission standards for coastal bathing waters.

Britain was rapped by the European Court over the state of the water at the two north west resorts in 1993 — and is now back in deep water.

The Commission is threatening to go back to court because the resorts still do not meet the legally-binding standards. A Commission spokesman said it had decided to send a "reasoned opinion" to the government — the final legal step before launching full court proceedings — if Britain cannot convince Brussels that it is meeting EU standards.

He added: "While substantial clean-up investments appear to have been made since 1993 recent monitoring results show that beaches around Blackpool continue to breach the standards set."

The latest action took the government by surprise. A No 10 spokesman expressed regret and said the UK was doing all it could to bring the beaches up to EU standards.

A spokesman for the Environment Agency said the problems could not be solved overnight. "The situation is very complicated and not something you can wave a magic wand over," he added.

Manchester Metro News 12 January 2000

Bread & butter reveals the bugs on British beaches

It's not just the water you have to watch out for on some of Britain's beaches. We found that the sand at two of the country's most popular resorts was contaminated with a type of bacteria more usually associated with human intestines – the products of which can find their way into the sea via coastal sewage outflow pipes. Our picnic-replicating investigations at Blackpool and Weston-super-Mare beaches picked up stomach-churning doses of *E coli* bacteria clinging to the test samples of bread and butter.

We sent microbiologists to 10 resorts around the English coastline armed with a supply of bread rolls, margarine and sterile sampling equipment. At various spots along each beach, they dropped bread rolls on to the sand, buttered side down. The soiled samples were then put in a sterile bag and taken to a laboratory to be tested for salmonella, campylobacter and *E coli* – food-poisoning bugs you wouldn't normally expect to find contaminating a beach.

Three out of eight samples taken from the beach around Blackpool's North and South Piers contained

high levels of *E coli*, and another two showed low levels of the bug. Two of the four samples from Weston-super-Mare's beach also revealed high *E coli* levels. Low levels of *E coli* contamination were found at Newquay and Bournemouth.

The most likely sources of the contamination are either pigeon and seagull droppings or seawater polluted with sewage. Blackpool failed to meet the EU mandatory standard for bathing-water quality in 1997, while Bournemouth and Weston-super-Mare met the mandatory standard but not the stricter guideline standard.

Samples taken at Littlehampton (near Brighton), Morecambe, Rhyl, Scarborough, Skegness, Torquay and Paignton beaches were all free of the food poisoning bacteria we tested for.

Holiday Which?
Autumn 1998

published by the
Consumers' Association,
2 Marylebone Rd, London
NW1 4DF
Tel: 0800 252 100

I LOVE BUTLINS

Rachel Johnson commends the celebrated Minehead resort

'HOW imaginative,' said friends en route to Tibet, or bound for a fortnight's water-colour course in a hilltop monastery in Umbria. 'How brave,' said other mothers as they headed to the wild unspoilt shores of Eigg or North Uist for shrimping on the beach with their children. 'How . . . amusing,' said those who were too shocked to say anything else.

Let's face it, a week's holiday in Butlins is not, currently, a destination of choice — not even for the working classes, who are supposed to love a knees-up by the seaside. Going to a holiday camp is simply not aspirational or exotic enough, not when we have so many holidays (sales of overseas packages have risen by 45 per cent in the 1990s), and the important thing seems to be not so much the frequency of our breaks as what they say about us.

We want to be thought fit and rugged, so we go canyoning in the Swiss Alps or white-water rafting in Colorado. We want to be thought elegant and tasteful, so we rent lush villas on Tuscan hillsides where we can eat the right sort of ham, or we 'summer' on Martha's Vineyard. We want to be thought understated, so we go to Scotland or Ireland and pretend not to mind the rain. But I didn't want to do any of these. One, I hadn't been asked; and two, I faced a five-day hole in July when, minus husband, I had nowhere to stay with my three children.

Butlins seemed the easy answer. It was only 12 miles away from my father's house on Exmoor; I could leave my children in the care of clotted-cream-fed Redcoats with comforting West Country accents, and have a blissful week lazing around my chalet with my book. 'I went to Butlins in Minehead for three years running when Hugo was little,' said my sister-in-law, 'and it was the only time I ever had a real rest.' I drove up the Exe Valley to Minehead with Caroline's words ringing in my ears ('You won't make any friends, but your children will love it; you have tea at 5 o'clock; it's bliss').

When you get to Minehead you can't miss Butlins, which has just had £58 million lavished on it by its owners, the Rank Organisation. Most of the money has gone on a vast tent called Skyline, which looks like an upturned udder and contains such treats as Harry Ramsden's, Burger King and various 'spaces' for Butlins' legendary Redcoats to perform (according to my brochure, this was where I was going to be able to 'relax and literally watch the incredible entertainment come to life around me').

When I checked in, the lady at the desk urged me to hurry straight to my assigned restaurant, Ocean Drive, which was staying open specially late — i.e., past 6 p.m. — to accommodate Monday's intake into the resort: a mere 8,000 campers. So we rushed to our chalet, dumped our bags, and rushed to the restaurant (when I say rushed, you must understand that getting from A to B in Butlins is a bit like getting around Heathrow — full of families pushing trolleys of luggage and buggies, arguing about who has got the keys and tickets: rushing takes time).

Our table, number 555, was already laid with rolls and butter, and a little stainless-steel teapot and teacups. The children were very excited when a server arrived with four jumbo cups of Pepsi for us to wash down the kids' menu, which read that night: main course, golden fishies, with french fries; sweet, lemon bombe; choice of carbonated drinks. As the server, Richard from Solihull, approached, I signalled at him wildly to take away the fizzy drinks, and asked him for some semi-skimmed milk for the children instead. 'Sorry,' he said, as he placed the brimming cups in front of each child. 'We don't do semi-skimmed milk. You're on holiday, aren't you? Can't you enjoy yourselves?'

I had just been wondering how on earth I was going to cope. We are not talking Michael Winner roughing it at Cliveden and complaining about the consistency of the freshly squeezed orange juice. It was the basic things. How were we going to cope with having our 'tea' at 5 p.m. and then eating nothing until the restaurant opened again for my breakfast sitting at 9 a.m.? And how were we all going to squeeze into rooms so small that the doors didn't shut when the beds were in, and the beds themselves were covered with oilcloth mattresses, as if we were about to give birth on them?

I felt despair rise from the pit of my stomach as I realised that all past travel —

trips to Israel, Africa, Peru etc. — had left me better equipped for one night in Bangkok than five days in Butlins. And then it dawned on me: this was about as foreign an experience as anyone who holidays abroad is ever likely to have. Forget ape-spotting in Uganda, diving off the Barrier Reef, even going to the moon in a Virgin rocket. Butlins at Minehead beats them all hands down in the competition for the Holiday with a Difference 1999.

So at every breakfast, lunch and tea — which was served on the dot of 5 p.m. — my children had their choice of carbonated drinks, and I had my choice of tea or coffee. I devoured my main courses which were always presented with a salad garnish or composite of leaves, while my children thoroughly enjoyed their Turkey Drummers and Bubble-gum Surprise.

In the evenings, we wandered around with the other families, pushing buggies and watching the shows in the Skyline Pavilion. My two-year-old clutched a bottle filled with teeth-rotting Ribena, just like all the other toddlers, and in the many shops and cafés my two older children whined and begged for me to buy them sweets and toys until I was driven to screaming, 'Do you want a smack? Just shut it or I'll smack your bottom!' very loudly, just like all the other tired mothers. I became quite used to the level of noise. All over the resort, but particularly in the swimming-pool — sorry, waterpark — Butlins plays the sort of music that sounds like people striking dustbin-lids together very fast. And I soon became used to the accommodation, much as Old Etonians find they adapt to life in prison.

In fact, I can highly recommend Butlins to women like me, who find they have nowhere to go for a few days and whose children demand incessant aural and visual stimulation. There are two other Butlins — in Bognor Regis and Skegness (known on-site as Boggie and Skeggie) —and the Redcoats tell me that there are the same fabulous, ear-splitting facilities in each, all upgraded last year at a cost of £138 million. May I just recommend that you arrive at your Family Entertainment Resort of Choice with the following items: cotton mattress-covers, available at John Lewis; towels and soap; a peppermill; a bedside light or powerful torch so that you can read in bed without using the eye-watering overhead lights, and, most important, earplugs so that you can sleep without being woken by the mother in the chalet next door screaming, 'If you hit your little brother again, I'm going to smack you one! Who do you think you are? Louise Woodward?' as mine did on most nights. Since we are all pretty good now at packing for those trekking holidays in Kathmandu, my Butlins Survival Kit should present little challenge to the seasoned traveller who wants a really exotic holiday next time round. So see you next year, then!

The author is a freelance journalist living in Brussels.

The Spectator 7 August 1999

Cheaper prices would attract more visitors

From: Name and address supplied.

Sir, – With reference to your article by Jo Makel (August 30), I can tell you exactly why visitor figures are down at tourist hotspots.

Every one prices itself utterly out of the market. Even allowing for the special reductions published in the *Yorkshire Post*, which, for the first time, only apply if one of the party is paying the full price.

As two senior citizens on a very limited income, in charge of a young grandson at weekends, who, for instance adores Harewood Adventure Playground, and myself who would love to see the Princess Royal's wedding dress, my husband and myself are confined to completely free venues which are excellent, but limited.

I would suggest that all participants drop the entrance price, and recoup the loss in increased attendance.

Yorkshire Post 2 September 1999

Come to Britain, a nation of oddballs

A NEW tourist guide to Britain was criticised yesterday for offending parts of the country.

Author Simon Henry, 29, an Oxford graduate, claimed A Tourist's Guide To The British provided 'invaluable insights into the regional and national stereotypes that characterise the modern world'. He described:

■ Yorkshiremen as monosyllabic 'dour skinflints' who only use the words 'no', 'can't' and 'won't'.

■ Glaswegians as 'unintelligible' drunks who 'prefer to spend their hard-earned social security money on McEwan's Export and unfiltered cigarettes'.

■ West Country folk as slow cider-guzzling yokels who drink excessive amounts of 'a noxious and highly intoxicating home-brewed cider, called scrumpy'.

■ Geordies as brown-ale addicts who 'pat their oversized stomachs with considerable pride'.

Mr Henry said Essex folk liked to spend their 'considerable wealth' on 'tasteless living' while Scots had a 'penchant for cross-dressing'.

Helen Holland, from the South West of England Regional Development Agency, said the book was disappointing. She added: 'Our inhabitants are anything but slow or stupid.'

But Mr Henry insisted: 'There are so many fantastic eccentricities about this country and this book is meant to be a celebration of that.'

News North West 29 February 2000

HAM

More than 600 tourists have booked guided coach tours to see rhubarb growing out of season in sheds in Wakefield, Yorkshire.
The Big Issue 10 January 2000

The winner of a brewery's competition for a trip anywhere in the world to see a football match chose to go to Leeds United, 16 miles from his home.
Promotions & Incentives Magazine January 1999

Trouble brewing for city tourists

WE had the pleasure of visiting the museums at Brewhouse Yard during the Bank Holiday, and after an enjoyable tour we eagerly looked forward to a refreshing cup of tea.

The immediate vicinity presented us with a number of bars offering tea and coffee but it would seem they are unable to supply a quick, fresh 'cuppa'.

After waiting 20 minutes for our order at our first port of call — plenty of staff and empty tables — we gave up and moved on.

The next bar was far from full and, having this time ordered one white wine, one tea and one coffee, we hoped for better things.

After ten minutes the glass of wine arrived and on enquiry we were told that there was a delay with the hot drinks as 'the machine had not been filled up'. Some five minutes later the coffee arrived and we asked again about the tea.

This time we were told they had run out of hot water. At this we gave up.

It does seem somewhat deplorable that this is the best Nottingham can do in its most popular tourist area.

SHEILA LYMN ROSE
Loughborough Road
Ruddington

Nottingham Evening Post 3 September 1999

Travel Etiquette

Follow our guide to social customs around the world to avoid embarrassment, tying yourself in knots – or worse

A nod is as good as a wink in Britain but it may not be in Greece or Bulgaria. Social etiquette in some countries can be baffling, but here are some tips on how to behave in various popular holiday destinations.

Table Manners

- In China, Hong Kong and Japan it's considered very bad luck to leave your chopsticks sticking out of a bowl of food.
- In Thailand it's good manners, when eating with a spoon and fork, to use the fork only to push food onto the spoon.
- In India, Indonesia and Singapore, where it is common to eat with your hands, licking your fingers is seen as bad manners.
- In India, Indonesia, Nepal and Singapore eating with your left hand is considered unhygienic.
- In Greece and Spain, outside the popular tourist areas, if you want to enjoy a convivial atmosphere at dinner, eat after 9pm.
- In Canada, New Zealand and the US most restaurants give free refills of coffee.
- In the US 'buffalo wings' on the menu usually means chicken wings.

Body Talk

- In Greece and Turkey to say 'no', people sometimes lift their heads back abruptly while raising their eyebrows.
- In Bulgaria a nod of the head is 'no' and a shake is 'yes'.
- In India, Indonesia, Japan, Korea, Malaysia, Morocco, Nepal and Thailand it's polite to take off your shoes before entering a house.
- In India, Malaysia, Nepal and Turkey pointing with a finger, if you are asking for directions, is rude – use the palm instead.

- In India a wobble of the head means 'yes' rather than 'maybe'.
- In Japan and Turkey blowing your nose in public is considered offensive.
- In India men may shake hands with other men but not with women. Instead, the greeting, as in Thailand, is a slight bow with palms together.
- In India, Indonesia, Nepal, Thailand and Turkey don't point with or show the sole of your foot or shoe to anyone.
- In Indonesia and Thailand never touch anyone's head, even a child's, as it is regarded as a sacred part of the body.
- In Japan you should greet people with a bow rather than shaking hands.

Over the Limit

- In New Zealand and South Africa shops don't sell alcohol on Sundays.
- In India the state of Gujarat has prohibition laws, but tourists can obtain a liquor permit allowing them to drink alcohol on holiday.
- In South Africa you may buy wine but not beer at supermarkets.
- In the US it's best to check before you drink alcohol in public areas or parks. The legal drinking age in the popular holiday states of Florida

and California is 21. Even if you are well into your 20s, it is advisable to carry ID, as you may be asked to prove your age in a bar. Minors are not allowed in bars – even to order non-alcoholic drinks.
- In the Czech Republic and Slovakia it's an offence to drink any alcohol and drive.
- In the Netherlands you can buy beer and wine at the age of 16, but you have to be at least 18 to buy spirits.
- In Egypt, Jordan, Morocco, Tunisia and Turkey drinking alcohol in common holiday destinations is OK, but it is better not to eat or drink in front of people who are fasting during the holy month of Ramadan, as it can be offensive.

Watch Your Mouth

- In Singapore smoking is banned in most public places (except air-conditioned pubs and discos) and so are eating and drinking on the subway system. The sale of chewing-gum is banned and you are not allowed to bring it into the country.
- In Hong Kong you can be fined for eating or drinking on the subway system and for smoking in indoor shopping arcades.
- Canada also has strict rules on smoking in public places.

- In the US smoking is a hazardous pursuit. If you want to smoke in New York, you should check the rules first, even in open spaces like sports stadiums. Smoking is banned in many public places, including large restaurants in New York and all restaurants and bars in California. If you want to light up, ask for a hotel room or hire-car designated for use by people who smoke.

Letter of The Law

- In Singapore you can be fined for jaywalking and for littering.
- Morocco, Russia and Tunisia don't allow the import or export of currency. All local currency must be spent or changed before leaving.
- In Kenya, Tanzania and Turkey it is an offence to destroy or deface local currency.
- In Switzerland pedestrians can be fined for crossing a road within 50m of a pedestrian crossing, bridge, or subway or against a red light.
- In India currency regulations are strict – you should change money at banks or legal foreign-exchange dealers only. Keep all receipts to prove you have obtained currency legally.
- In Japan you will need a doctor's letter if you want to take paracetamol, Sudafed, or nasal sprays, such as Vicks, into the country.
- In the US and Turkey it's an offence to insult the national flag. In the US you should put your hand on your heart and take your hat off during the national anthem.
- In Thailand you have to stand up when the national anthem is played in the cinema.

Religious Observance

- In India, Nepal, Sri Lanka and Thailand don't touch any statues of deities in Hindu or Buddhist temples and never point your feet towards an image of Buddha.
- In Sri Lanka and Thailand women should never touch Buddhist monks and should avoid sitting next to them.
- In Thailand you should take your shoes off before entering a Buddhist temple. Images of Buddha, even at tourist sites, should not be photographed without permission.
- In the Czech Republic, Israel and Poland men must wear skullcaps in some synagogues and Jewish cemeteries. Women should keep arms and legs covered.
- In Greece, Romania and Russia men should wear long trousers and women should wear long-sleeved dresses, in Orthodox churches. In Russia men should remove hats and women should wear headscarves.
- In Egypt, Morocco, Tunisia and Turkey, non-Muslims should not go into mosques or cemeteries unless they are tourist sights. If you do enter a mosque, always take your shoes off. Don't go in if a service is in progress. Try not to walk in front of someone who is praying. Both men and women should keep their legs and shoulders covered; women should also cover their heads.
- In Egypt, Jordan, Morocco, Tunisia and Turkey, where prayers may take place anywhere, you should not be embarrassed if prayers are being said in front of you – for example, by a shopkeeper on his premises.

Confused? You Will Be

- In Australia a 'station' is a large farm, 'lollies' are sweets and a 'milk bar' is a corner shop.
- In South Africa a 'café' is a general store where you can't sit down for a cup of coffee. If someone says 'just now', they mean later, but 'now, now' means immediately. A 'robot' is a traffic light.
- In New Zealand a 'dairy' is a general store.
- In the Netherlands a 'coffee shop' in Amsterdam is a place whose main business is selling cannabis: look out for a hemp leaf on the shop window.
- In Japan many restaurant toilets are unsegregated. Also make sure you change into specially reserved toilet slippers before using the toilet in a Japanese home or youth hostel. Baths are for soaking in, not washing – rinse off all soap before you get in.
- In Spain when someone talks about midday (media dia) they are referring not to 12 noon but to lunch-time – some time between 2pm and 4pm.
- In the US the 'first floor' is the ground floor, while 'cookies' are biscuits and 'biscuits' are scones. Dates are formatted mm/dd/yy, while in Canada dates are usually written in the same way as in Britain (dd/mm/yy).
- In Japan the years are often dated by the number of years the Emperor has reigned.
- In Thailand they are well into the 26th century.

Holiday Which? Autumn 1998
Consumers' Association, 2 Marylebone Rd,
London NW1 4DF Tel: 0800 252 100

What a Handful

In Greece, Spain, and Turkey the fig gesture (fist with thumb protruding between index and middle fingers) is considered very rude

In Egypt the right hand over the heart means 'no, thank you'

In Greece an open palm and extended fingers (like a 'five' sign) can be insulting

In Japan, Korea, and Mexico making a circle or semi-circle with forefinger and thumb is a symbol for money; in France the same gesture means something is worthless; in Brazil it is very rude; in the US it means OK

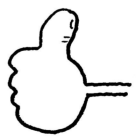

In Morocco and parts of the Middle East the thumbs-up sign is an obscenity

Tipping

How much should you pay a porter or slip a steward? Here's our guide to global gratuities

For many people, tip is a four-letter word, producing embarrassment, guilt, or irritation for all concerned. You can feel a social outcast for not tipping in places where it is almost a national pastime, such as the US. Equally excruciating can be a tip where it is not expected – in Australia, for instance. Our table gives our guidelines on whom to tip, where, how much, and when, in some of the most popular holiday destinations. Below are some general tips.

Make sure that a service charge hasn't already been included before you leave extra. It may be listed on the bill under 'grat' or 's/c'. If your credit card slip is left open, don't automatically assume that service hasn't already been charged. Check before you sign.

Double check that you're not paying a percentage of the tax as well – the tip should be based on the pre-tax bill.

If you pay with plastic, you may prefer to leave a cash tip, as the waiting staff are more likely to get this.

On cruises, check the tour operator's brochure first. Some operators, such as Swan Hellenic and Thomson, include the tips in the price. Most lines, however, recommend tipping at the end of a trip, though this can be an expensive business – around £2 per person per day for waiters and cabin stewards. Service charges of up to 15 per cent are sometimes added to bar bills.

We found no mention of tips in the main tour operators' all-inclusive brochures. When our inspectors visited all-inclusive resorts in Europe this year, it was not common practice to tip, and some resorts discourage staff from accepting tips.

Where the service charge has been automatically included in restaurant prices, as in many European countries, it can be difficult to refuse to pay the charge if you feel that service was unsatisfactory. In Germany and Austria, for example, the only way to express dissatisfaction is by not tipping (in both countries, tips are expected on top of the compulsory service charge). In France and Belgium, however, you are entitled to withhold payment of part of the bill if you feel that the service was not satisfactory.

	Restaurants
Australia	No service charge. Tip 5-10% only for exceptional service.
Austria	10-15% service charge usually included in menu prices. For good service, it is customary to leave a small tip.
Belgium	Around 20% service charge usually included in menu prices. For good service, leave a discretionary cash tip as well.
Canada	Sometimes a 15% service charge added to bill. Where service charge is not added, leave a tip of approx 15%.
Caribbean	Antigua, Barbados, St Lucia – No service charge. Tip 10%.
Cyprus	10% service charge included in menu prices.
France	10-15% service charge included in all menu prices. It is customary also to tip a few francs as a mark of appreciation.
Germany	10% service charge usually included in menu prices. For good service, you can also leave a tip of up to 10%. Tip as you pay the bill, rather than leaving it on the table when you go.
Greece	10% service charge usually added. Tip Dr200-500 for good service.
India	Service charge not usually added, so tip 8-15% in tourist restaurants, a few rupees in smaller places. In bigger restaurants, tips form about 80% of waiters' take-home pay.
Ireland	10-15% service charge sometimes added to the bill. If not added, tip 10% for good service.
Italy	10-12% usually added to bill. If not added, leave 5-10%.
Malta	No service charge. Tip 10%.
Morocco	10% service charge usually applies in restaurants but not in cafés. If not, tip up to 10%. Waiters rely heavily on tips.
Netherlands	No service charge. Tip 10-15% for good service.
New Zealand	No service charge. Tipping not expected but becoming more widespread, so may tip 5-10% for exceptional service.
Poland	No service charge. Tip 10%.
Portugal	No service charge. Tip 5-10% for good service.
Singapore	10% service charge usually added to bill. Tipping not expected (even where no service charge is added).
Spain	Service charge of around 15% (varying between regions) included in menu prices. Leave a small tip (2-10%) for good service.
Switzerland	15% service charge included in menu prices. Extra tips not expected.
Thailand	Service charge not usually added. Tipping is polite - the amount depends on the level of service and type of restaurant. Waiters rely on tips.
Tunisia	Service charge not usually added. Customary to tip 10-15% for good service. Waiters rely on tips.
Turkey	Service charge not usually added. Tip 10%, even where service charge has been added.
USA	Service charge included only for large parties. A tip of 15% (20% for excellent service) expected everywhere - calculate by doubling the tax, usually listed separately on bill. Waiters rely heavily on tips.

	Hotels	Taxis	Other
Australia	No service charge added and no tips expected.	Tip not expected.	Tipping is not part of the culture.
Austria	10-15% service charge. Tip porters Sch10-20 and maids from Sch20, depending on length of stay	Tip Sch10-20.	Some hotels operate a 'piggy-bank' system, where you leave a single tip on departure (from around Sch200 per week), which is shared among all staff.
Belgium	Approximately 20% service charge. For good service, tip porters and room service approximately BFr50.	Tip not expected.	Toilet attendants may expect BFr10.
Canada	No service charge. Tip porters around C$1 per piece of luggage.	Tip 15%.	
Caribbean	10% service charge in most hotels. Leave extra discretionary tips for good service.	Tip 10%	
Cyprus	10% service charge. Small change for porters and cleaners is appreciated.	Tip appreciated but not always expected.	
France	12-15% service charge. Leave small tips (Fr5-10) for staff as a mark of appreciation.	Tip Fr5-10.	Also leave tips (Fr5-10) for door staff and cinema ushers.
Germany	No service charge. Tips discretionary for good service.	Tip depending on service – 10% is generous.	Tipping throughout Germany is purely voluntary and to be used as an expression of particular satisfaction.
Greece	8-18% service charge on some aspects of the bill, e.g. room service and phone calls. Tip porters up to Dr500 per case.	Tip around Dr100-200 for good service.	
India	Service charge not usually added. Tip porters and room service waiters Rs10-100, depending on service and class of hotel.	Tips not necessary, although more likely to be expected in the tourist taxis rather than the yellow-top metered ones.	Site attendants and many other staff in tourist destinations sometimes expect Rs10-20. Tour guides sometimes expect up to Rs100-200.
Ireland	Sometimes 10-15% service charge. Tips discretionary for good service, eg IRE£1 for a porter.	Tip 10% for good service.	
Italy	No service charge. Tip discretionary for good service, e.g. L3-4,000 for a porter and L10-20,000 for a maid per week.	Tip approximately L3,000.	
Malta	No service charge. Tip hotel staff, e.g. Lm0.5-1.5 for room service, Lm1 for a porter.	Tip Lm0.5-1, depending on journey length.	
Morocco	10% service charge on room service. Tip porters and waiters for good service, between Dh5 and Dh50.	Tip up to Dh5 on short journeys; 5-10% of fare on longer ones.	It is also customary to tip a few dirhams for car-parking services.
Netherlands	No service charge. Leave tips only for good service, e.g. G3-5 for a porter, G2-10 for a maid.	Tip 10%.	
New Zealand	No service charge. Tipping not expected.	Tipping not expected.	Tipping is not part of the culture and is the exception rather than the rule.
Poland	No service charge. Tip porters around Zl5.	Tip 10%.	Toilet attendants expect Zl1.
Portugal	No service charge. Tips discretionary for good service, e.g. Esc500 for a porter.	Tip approximately 10%.	No established culture of tipping. Leaving tips is discretionary.
Singapore	10% service charge. Tipping not expected.	Tipping not expected.	
Spain	Service charge included in prices (amount varies between regions). Tips discretionary for good service, e.g. Pta100 for a porter.	Tip approximately 5%.	No established culture of tipping. Leaving tips is discretionary.
Switzerland	15% service charge. Tipping not expected.	Fares include service. Can round up the bill, but tips not expected.	
Thailand	No service charge. Tip staff Bt20-50.	Tip Bt50-100.	
Tunisia	No service charge. Tip porters around TD1 per case and maids around TD10 per week.	Round up the fare.	Small change is handy as a donation when visiting mosques.
Turkey	15% service charge. Tip staff, e.g. TL2-5 for a porter.	Tips not expected, except for long journeys or full-day hire.	Tip TL5 in Turkish baths.
USA	No service charge. Tip $1 for a porter, $1-2 for a maid per night.	Tip 10-20% (more where bags are carried).	Tip cloakroom staff $1 per item, and valet-parking staff $2.

Holiday Which? Winter 1999
Consumers' Association, 2 Marylebone Rd, London NW1 4DF. Tel 0800 252 100

Post-holiday depression can ruin a break. But there can be life after a vacation

Crash landing

IT'S A RECURRING NIGHTMARE. You come back from holiday, traffic seems worse, house seems smaller, paperwork has bred in your absence and it seems as if you never went away. Can we avoid those horrible post-holiday blues? Unfortunately, probably not. But there are steps we can take to ease the return to reality.

'If you feel that bad after time off, it's almost too late,' says Andrew West, an occupational psychologist in London. 'Before you leave, you need to plan your return to work and everyday life just the way you plan holidays so that they become more of a balance between work and life.'

West suggests leaving your home and office tidy before you go, so that there won't be an overwhelming number of tasks to do when you get home. 'If you have the luxury of a cleaner, have them come in while you're away so you don't come back to piles of washing. Similarly, resist the temptation to put off projects at work for when you get back. Returning to a clean desk makes a

big difference in your outlook.'

West also says that an abrupt change in our bodies' physical schedule can make coming home difficult. He recommends returning at least a day before you need to, to allow your body to readjust.' If you've been staying up late and getting up late and you come home the day before you return to work, forcing yourself to get up early the next morning makes everything harder.'

Because rejoining the humdrum can be so difficult, you may need to remind yourself of what you like about home. 'There's always something good about coming home, even if it's only that there are no mosquitoes,' says Marie Mosely, a business psychologist. 'It's important to tell yourself you are going to enjoy being home because what's the alternative? You're going to be there until you go away again.'

Mosely thinks that part of the reason people feel blue when they come back is because they don't take full advantage of being away. 'People frequently waste the first few days of their holiday sleeping a lot because they focus only on getting there,' she says. 'You can help avoid that by changing your mindset before you go. Think about how you're going to have a good time, sleep well, feel refreshed and make the most of the time you have. If you actively fill your days, you will avoid feeling as if the holiday never happened.'

Although feeling let down after time away is probably par for the course, those feelings may intensify if the time away has been

Travel Matters © Carel Press

stressful or disappointing. Some negativity can be avoided by considering in advance your travelling companions' expectations. Mosely says that different ways of managing time can lead to friction. 'If one person is keen on leaving the hotel room early every day and the other wants to lie in, it can be stressful for both,' she says.

Most holiday frustrations arise from unmet expectations and not being prepared for disappointment. 'People often have high expectations but there are bound to be disappointments – with the weather, the accommodation or even because of friction with family members,' says Paul Gilbert, professor of clinical psychology at Derby University. 'The more we set up things to be wonderful, then the more we are disappointed when they're not. But if you get upset over every little thing, your bad mood can spoil the holiday.'

What if even after all that careful planning you come home and you just can't shake the blues? Psychologists seem to agree that feeling out of sorts for a week or

two is perfectly natural, but if gloomy feelings continue or worsen, it could be more than post-holiday blues.

'If people have a very strong desire to escape, that's often an

---

There's always something good about coming home, even if it's only that there are no mosquitoes

---

indication that there may be a deeper, underlying problem,' says Gilbert. 'Holidays can be times when families spend a lot of time together and conflicts come to the fore.' He says that holidays can trigger awareness of a big problem like a failing marriage and then people come back and fall into depression.

But he cautions to distinguish between the blues and full-scale depression. 'When we feel down because we are disappointed or mourning something, it's all about the world feeling empty and us not being very happy with it,' Gilbert explains. 'As we move into depression, our inner selves begin

to feel empty and we may feel inadequate or that we have failed.' Disrupted sleep patterns, loss of appetite, a sense of hopelessness and feeling very down about yourself are all possible signs of depression that might warrant professional help. Otherwise Gilbert recommends talking over your post-holiday blues with friends – chances are they feel the same way and can help you readjust.

Minor feelings of dissatisfaction can be put to good use. 'Try to work out what seems so terrible about coming back,' says Gilbert. 'Are you feeling blue about the holiday or what you've come back to?' The holiday itself may be the problem.

'If you feel bad after a holiday, you need to reappraise what your life's about and if you're taking the appropriate relaxation,' says Andrew West. 'The worst thing is to spend a fortune on a holiday, not enjoy it and then come back and pay for it.'

Emily Laurence Baker
The Guardian 18 August 1998

Ward off the blues

☀ Keep a memento at hand so you can relive holiday moments.

☀ Schedule meetings, business trips or other work to boost your motivation.

☀ Leave your desk and house as neat as possible so that coming home doesn't feel oppressive.

☀ Plan a small treat for when you return so that you have something to look forward to.

☀ Expect disappointment but vow to enjoy the holiday anyway.

INDEX

Entries in **bold** refer to main sections.

Published by Carel Press Ltd
4 Hewson St, Carlisle CA2 5AU
Tel 01228 538928, *Fax 591816*
Carel_Press@compuserve.com

This collection ©2000 Carel Press
First published: May 2000
Adviser: Christine A Shepherd
Cover design: Arthur Procter
Cover: Venice the day after the Pink Floyd Concert. Photo: Arici/Grazianeri
Back cover: Raleigh International
Readers: Ann Batey, Debbie Maxwell, Paula Stokes

Printed by MFP Ltd, Manchester

Thanks to Carlisle Library; Social Science Library, Manchester Central Library

We wish to thank all those writers, editors, photographers, cartoonists, artists, press agencies and wire services who have given permission to reproduce copyright material. Every effort has been made to trace copyright holders of material but in a few cases this has not been possible. The publishers would be glad to hear from anyone who has not been consulted.

Environmental Information
The book is printed on 100% recycled paper which is made entirely from printed waste, & is not re-bleached. Using recycled paper saves trees & water, & reduces air pollution & landfill.

CIP Data: A catalogue record for this book is available from the British Library

Additional copies of this book, for individual student use, and as an alternative to photocopying, may be purchased at a discount from the publishers.

ISBN 1-872365-66-3

> ' **Travel, in the younger sort, is a part of education; in the elder, a part of experience.** '
>
> *Francis Bacon 1561 - 1626*